HIDDEN
HISTORY
of
DETROIT

HIDDEN
HISTORY
of
DETROIT

Amy Elliott Bragg

Charleston London

THE
History
PRESS

Published by The History Press
Charleston, SC 29403
www.historypress.net

Copyright © 2011 by Amy Elliott Bragg

First published 2011
Second printing 2012
Third printing 2012
Fourth printing 2013

Manufactured in the United States

ISBN 978.1.60949.269.4

Library of Congress Cataloging-in-Publication Data

Bragg, Amy Elliott.
Hidden history of Detroit / Amy Elliott Bragg.
p. cm.
Includes bibliographical references.
ISBN 978-1-60949-269-4
1. Detroit (Mich.)--History. I. Title.
F574.D457B73 2011
977.4'34--dc23
2011036376

For General Friend Palmer,
and for Scott.

Contents

CONTENTS

ACKNOWLEDGEMENTS

Huge gratitude to all of the following:
The Burton Historical Collection at the Detroit Public Library, for tireless stewardship of its incredible, illuminating archives and endless help for clueless researchers like me.

John Notarianni, for carefully made cocktails and dreamy late-night porch talks about Gabriel Richard.

Emily Eagle, for her smart, insightful reading and the kind of creative advice that only a radio producer can give.

Dan Austin, for recruiting me into service, for sharing priceless finds, for believing in my blog early on and for eagle-eyed editing.

Readers, friends and followers of nighttraintodetroit.com.

The History Press, especially Joe Gartrell, my commissioning editor.

Paul, Patti and Stephen Bragg, my fabulous new family-in-law.

Joan and Sy Ginsberg, my parents, for love, support and an education.

And my outrageously great husband, for his wisdom, his patience, his kindness, his generosity and his jokes.

INTRODUCTION

When I told my dad that I was writing a book about Detroit history, he asked, "What kind of history? Like the kind you read in books?" Yeah, I said. Basically.

"So what's the point? If it's already in a book?" Then he asked if I was going to write about prohibition, which, as it turns out, is a common question people ask when they find out you're writing a book about Detroit history. And I did write about prohibition. Just not the prohibition that people remember.

My dad didn't realize it at the time, but he hit a nerve I have about writing history: by definition, hasn't history already been written? And doesn't that make me a hack?

I started writing about history because I didn't know anything about it. I had just moved back to my hometown, Farmington Hills, from Milwaukee. I did it for a pretty good reason—my then boyfriend, now husband—but once I got here, I had some feelings to deal with—teenage feelings. What did it mean to live in the suburbs again? What was this freakish place I had come from, with its acres of weedy parking lots, fake-looking front lawns, brigades of high-shine SUVs and miles of strip malls stretching into the sunset? And where had Farmington Hills come from? And how did it fit into the sprawling galaxy of cities, townships and villages that enveloped its hard-as-a-marble core of Detroit?

Before I started writing about Detroit history, I thought Detroit history went like this: French fur traders founded it, something something something, there was a fire at some point, then Henry Ford started making cars and then Detroit got really big! Something about prohibition and the Purple Gang, and then the riots in the '60s, when white people left town and made the suburbs. And now today, it's getting better, sort of, but there are still a lot of empty buildings. And a lot of suburbs.

It's not that everything I knew about Detroit history was wrong. But it was certainly incomplete and hasty. Detroit sometimes forgets that there was ever a time before the automobile, or that it's one of the oldest and most perpetually influential cities in the Midwest: battle ground of the War of 1812, capital city of the Michigan Territory, last stop on the Underground Railroad and then, variously, Stove City, Dry Dock City, Cigar City, Salt City and Pharma City decades before the Motor City had motors to move it.

The suburbs, too, existed and prospered long before the combustion engine. Farmington was established by Quakers in 1824. Nathan Power, Farmington's founding father, is buried in its tiny Quaker Cemetery next to his first wife and five-year-old daughter, who both died during the cholera outbreak of 1832.

History gave me a way into Farmington and, ultimately, Detroit. I traipsed through cemeteries to meet the people I was reading about, visited the landmarks they left behind and blogged about everything I turned up. Some of my reports from the field were obvious. Others were obscure. I gravitated toward mysteries, rumors, legends, ghost stories, funny stories and stories about people drinking. Did you know that when Mad Anthony Wayne (victor of the Battle of Fallen Timbers and namesake of Wayne County) was exhumed from his grave in Erie, Pennsylvania, his bones were boiled in a big cauldron, stuffed into two saddlebags and then taken overland to his family's cemetery in Radnor? People say that his ghost wanders U.S. 322 looking for the bones that fell out of the packs. Have you heard the one about the 1817 Conant & Mack Company expedition to Pontiac, where Lewis Cass, Solomon Sibley, David McKinstry and Alexander Macomb snuck into a gristmill and had an impromptu flour-grinding competition? Some say that they gave the winner the first mayorship of Detroit. Then they fake-arrested a homesteader for not drinking with them and fake-sentenced him to death. He fainted. When he revived, they plied him with apologies and gifts, and he said that he would go through it all over again.

Depending on whom you ask, I became terrific fun at parties or a total bore at parties. And through it all, there were the books—always the books (and library monographs and digital archives). And with the books was the creeping fear that I was just regurgitating what people had already written about—you know, in books.

But as I started working on my own book, I started thinking about the history of those history books, especially the two I loved the most, *History of Detroit and Michigan* and *Early Days in Detroit*, published in 1884 and 1906, respectively. Who had written them and why? And how did they look at the world? Were they informed by what the authors remembered of the city or what they saw coming for the city in the future? What moved them? Where did they see themselves in the portraits they drew of Detroit?

At John King, a majestic used bookstore in an old glove factory just off the Lodge Freeway, I found a copy of *City of Destiny*, written by George Washington Stark in 1943, during the Arsenal of Democracy years. The book—signed by the author, it turned out—was stuffed with newspaper clippings about Stark, a columnist for the *Detroit Free Press* and a self-described "old-timer."

Stark was born in 1884, and he remembered pre-automotive Detroit, a muddy place full of spooked horses and barn fires but also peace, quiet, gentility and tree-lined avenues. He wrote *City of Destiny*, a treasure box of city history told fast and loose from Cadillac to press date, as a project in context. How did Detroit's destiny lead from the rough river shores of Fort Pontchartrain in 1701 to the nerve center of World War II and one of the biggest cities in America? He wrote:

> *Since Cadillac came, the community, as outpost, village, town and city, has experienced both travail and triumph, each in heaping measure. It has endured fire and famine and pestilence and somehow survived them all. It has withstood rioting and the shock of savage assault and it has recovered from the humiliation of a craven military surrender. It has*

been rocked by political scandal and intrigue, but in every instance, it has quickly recovered its prestige.

These defeats and frustrations have been more than balanced by the triumphs. Or, if you prefer, THE TRIUMPH, for its present eminence is the result of no recent industrial development. Rather, it is the sequence of a long progression of men and events.

History writers sought similar context as the curtains closed on the nineteenth century and Detroit approached its 1901 bicentennial. The pioneers who had come to the city with the advent of the steamboat in the 1820s were beginning to die off. The fortunes of Detroit were no longer tied to farming, fishing or the fur trade but instead relied on large-scale manufacturing and heavy industry. The streets were electrically lit at night; crowded with bicycles, pedestrians, buggies with motors on them and horse and coaches; and crisscrossed with streetcars both electrified and horse-drawn. Houses that had been built by French families a century earlier were torn down. Houses that had been built by captains of industry thirty or forty years prior were torn down, too. General Friend Palmer collected his reminiscences of the days of steamboat captain-kings and the old stalwarts who hung out on the patio of Sheldon & Rood bookstore and gossiped all summer about Indian concomitance and Indian raids. Silas Farmer started his encyclopedia of early Detroit. And as the 200th anniversary of Detroit's founding approached, historical committees sprang to action, and Detroiters became enraptured with the story of their knightly founder, the Sieur de Cadillac, his hardy voyageurs and his glamorous frontier wife. Reenactments, pageants, parades and memorials were inescapable.

It's 2011, and I think I missed the latest "where we've been/where we're going" check-in by ten years. When we celebrated the tricentennial in 2001, I was a junior in high school and not at all aware that Detroit was celebrating a tricentennial.

But now is a good time (is there ever a bad time?) to take up the voyage again. When Detroiters talk about history today, it's often to make sense of Detroit's "big mess": a dwindling population, high unemployment, a hollowed-out economy, acres of empty property and an infrastructure desperately in need of repair. How did this happen after we spent half of the twentieth century on top of the world?

Detroit's history can do so much more than that, though. There's a lot of joy in these old halls (I giggle a lot when I work on this stuff) and plenty to celebrate. There are role models and stories of mortal hubris— like the hot spur and boy wonder Stevens T. Mason, who went toe to toe with the State of Ohio and President Andrew Jackson to deliver Michigan to statehood and whose ambition created a statewide network of roads, railways and canals, effecting a gaping hole in the new state's economy. And there's a reason Re-Elect Pingree posters pop up all over town during election years.

"Detroit is opulent and generous," wrote George Washington Stark in his introduction to *City of Destiny*. I believe that to be true. To that I would add tenacious. I think the best lesson of Detroit history, end to end, is that this dynamic city, against all odds, will persevere. It will change, perhaps even drastically. But it will rise.

So yes, this is a history book, full of the kind of history you read about in history books. But I have strived to bring Detroit history to life a little—to introduce you to people I love, to make you laugh and to illuminate a city that you may not have realized was ever here.

I hope it gives you, as it has given me, a way home.

HISTORIANS

Before we get started, there are three people you need to meet. Two of them created—through sweat, drudgery, obsession, near-pathological attention to detail and humorless dispositions—the definitive canon of Detroit history before 1900.

The third, my wild card pick, brings a needed dose of personality to any picture of the early city. And I like him. I kind of want to hug him.

I know it's a little funny to start a book with the bibliography, and of course there have been dozens of other history writers and hundreds of other books. But almost everyone who writes about early Detroit starts with the same basic sources: Silas Farmer's *History of Detroit and Michigan* and Clarence M. Burton's Alexandria-like archive of original documents at the Detroit Public Library.

I'll be quoting them so much that it just doesn't seem polite to invite them to the party without proper introduction. So, here they are.

THE MAPMAKER

When Silas Farmer died suddenly in 1902, one obituary eulogized him as a particular breed of genius—the kind of person born with "the infinite capacity for taking pains." It was a genius, the writer argued, that Silas Farmer had inherited from his father. But Silas's genius was not the only thing his father passed down to him.

Silas Farmer, author of *History of Detroit and Michigan*. *Burton Historical Collection, Detroit Public Library.*

There was the family business, for one. Though he had been a teacher in Albany, New York, John Farmer came to Detroit as an entrepreneur—he wanted to make maps. A skilled surveyor and draftsman, Farmer had done some work for another publisher on contract, sketching out maps of the Michigan Territory from surveyors' plats. But the subsequent pamphlets took forever to publish, and he didn't get credit for his work in the final product. So John Farmer decided to strike out on his own. In 1825, Farmer's own map of Michigan became the first published map of the territory.

John Farmer's maps were exacting and lavishly detailed, and new arrivals to Detroit and Michigan snapped them up by the score. Bookstores stocked thousands of his pocket guides, and they were *still* hard to come by; before traveling into the wilds of the territory, new settlers would go door to door, looking for someone to sell them a secondhand copy. Farmer eventually taught himself how to engrave, cutting out a middleman in the publishing process. He was also a keen marketer, conducting direct mail campaigns and

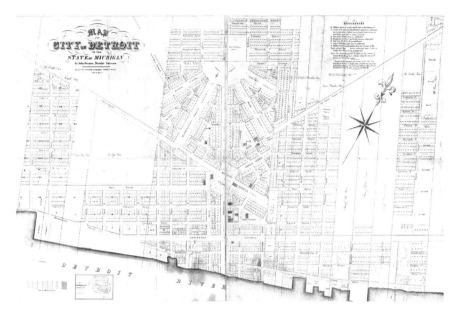

John Farmer's maps, like this one of Detroit in 1835, were the first and best maps available of the Michigan Territory. *Map of the City of Detroit in the State of Michigan, 1835, by John Farmer, District Surveyor; Eng. by C.B. & J.R. Graham Lithographers, New York. Library of Congress Geography and Map Division.*

soliciting celebrity testimonials from political luminaries such as Lewis Cass and William Woodbridge.

Silas, born in Detroit in 1839, took an early interest in the business and took over completely in 1859 when John Farmer died unexpectedly at age sixty-one—of overwork, most people assumed.

"It seemed to me that the steam engine within him must sooner or later wear him out," General Friend Palmer wrote of John Farmer. "And it did."

Silas inherited that steam engine heart from his father. Whether it was the ethic of a workhorse that doesn't quit until it drops dead or a genetic predisposition to heart problems, Silas died at nearly the same age, 63, and presumably of the same ailment.

In 1874, with business at the Farmer Company steady and successful, Silas decided to pursue a long-held curiosity. For the country's centennial celebration, he would publish a comprehensive history of the city of Detroit.

Almost immediately, Silas knew that he was in over his head. But like the hundreds of researchers, writers and hobbyists who came after him, he did not give up. Instead, he got swept away.

It's hard to express how grateful I feel for the work that Silas Farmer did. The nature of historical research was, obviously, completely different in Silas Farmer's time, and while it is nice to just pop open my laptop and start downloading PDFs of his delightful neighborhood souvenirs from the Internet Archive, I'm not even talking about computers.

Silas had no Burton Collection (more on that in a minute) from which to draw. He sent form letters to churches, newspapers, businesses and government agencies across the Midwest and from San Francisco to New York City, Dublin and Paris soliciting records, account books and registries. He called on small-town historical societies, archives and libraries. He met with institutional Detroiters to pick their brains and rifle through their papers.

In his foreword to the first edition of *History of Detroit and Michigan*— published ten years after his research began and at a personal cost of about $17,000 (more than $400,000 today, adjusted for inflation)—he wrote of his research:

> *The tracing of some facts has been like the tracking of a hare; again and again it has been necessary to go back on the path, and renew the search, and at times, while rummaging in the garrets of old French houses and later dwellings, amid the dust and must of a century, I have almost forgotten to what age I belonged, and have for a time lived in the midst of past regimes.*

History of Detroit and Michigan is, first and foremost, exhaustive. It's about one thousand pages long and illustrated with hundreds of gorgeous Farmer Company engravings of houses, cityscapes, historic views and documents. It's not a chronological history of Detroit from 1701 onward; instead, it's a topical work, covering discrete subjects (military affairs, health systems, aldermanic wards and visits from famous people) in encyclopedic detail.

This is the history book of a mapmaker. The level of detail is painstaking—a list of public drinking fountains and the year they were erected, for instance, or a brief passage about "Old Joe," the fire department's Newfoundland dog—but every small, functional fact comes together to form a graceful picture of the whole. Silas wrote:

A good history is like a landscape, in that many things are brought at once within the range of vision; and it should resemble a photograph, preserving those minute points which give character to the subject...Stars of the first magnitude are easily found: It is the little asteroids that escape observation, and as these are discovered various planetary disturbances are explained.

The book was a success, selling thousands of copies around the world. Silas revised and reissued it in 1889 and again in 1894.

He lived a quiet and strictly Christian life. A founding member of the Detroit Young Men's Christian Society and a board member at the Central Methodist Church for twenty-five years, Silas wrote poetry about temperance and living a morally upright life. And he worked and worked and worked, serving as city historiographer and writing pamphlets, gazetteers and street guides about Detroit, its surrounding communities and the state of Michigan. For *An Illustrated History and Souvenir of Detroit*, a little tour book, Silas counted the steps (two hundred of them) as he climbed to the top of Old City Hall to capture the breathtaking view.

Silas oversaw historical activities for the Detroit bicentennial festivities in 1901. A year later, he died in his sleep. His only child, Arthur, took over the Farmer Company, but he didn't have his father's gift for it, and he went out of business in a few years, granting all of the company's engraving plates to Clarence M. Burton.

My copy of *History of Detroit* is a faithful 1969 reissue from Gale Research Company. Time after time—especially when I feel lazy—I crack it open and sit for a while with Silas, wandering the endless alleys and byways of his Detroit. Stern, puritanical Silas still manages to slip in a joke (like when he calls early citizen Peter Audrain "clerk of everything from time immemorial") and a little romance ("The glory of the ancient market-days has departed. The black-eyed, olive-skinned maidens, in short petticoats, from the Canada shore, no longer bring 'garden-sauce and greens,' the French ponies amble not over our paved streets, and little brown-bodied carts no longer throng the marketplace").

Like John Farmer's maps before it, Silas's *History* gave Detroiters a new opportunity to get intimately acquainted with their city. Nothing like it had ever been attempted before in the city; nothing like it since has ever been accomplished.

THE LIBRARIAN

Clarence Monroe Burton was born in Whiskey Diggings, a California gold rush town, in November 1853. His parents—Charles Seymour Burton, a doctor, and Annie Monroe Burton, a poet—had come to California in a wagon train from Battle Creek, Michigan, earlier that year. Whatever fortune they sought, they must not have found it, because they packed up and set out for home on the steamer *Yankee Blade* the following fall.

On October 1, lost in fog off the coast of Point Arguello, the *Yankee Blade* struck a rock. The boat broke in two. Annie Burton, with baby Clarence on her hip and pieces of gold sewn into her skirts, tried to jump from the ship into a waiting lifeboat. She missed her mark, and the two of them plunged into the rocky Pacific waters, but someone in the lifeboat grabbed Annie and pulled her and her son aboard.

Hundreds of passengers drowned when the *Yankee Blade* sank. All of the Burtons survived. By 1855, they were back in New York. These are

Clarence M. Burton. *Burton Historical Collection, Detroit Public Library.*

auspicious beginnings for a man who would grow up to be—by most standards of polite society—kind of a bore.

The Burton family returned to Michigan, to the farm town of Hastings (where Charles Burton started a newspaper, the *Hastings Banner*—still published today). Clarence Burton grew up, went to the University of Michigan, got in trouble with the dean for letting some circus animals loose on campus and graduated—though he refused to pay extra for the actual diploma—with a law degree.

Burton moved to Detroit in 1874 to clerk for a law firm. His wife, Harriet, and their firstborn, Agnes, stayed behind while he worked side jobs and slept in the office—he was only making about $100 a year. Still, he found spare change to snap up a book or two.

I'm not sure when Burton's part-time history habit became a driving force in his life, but I imagine it happened slowly, book by book, document by document, mystery by slow-burning mystery. It's a rewarding pursuit that way.

In 1885, Clarence, Harriet and their (now five) children moved from a small house in the neighborhood of Corktown to a slightly bigger house on Brainard Street off Cass Avenue, about a mile from the center of the city. The Burtons needed room for their growing brood, of course, and when Clarence Burton added a third story to the house, it was partly to gain a few more bedrooms for the children. But it also gave Burton a large study to call his own, as well as a space to store his growing collection of books.

His son Frank's earliest memories were of the study and of his father's exacting and methodical way of cultivating his library:

> *Up at a good hour in the morning, he ate a hearty breakfast and left at once for the office...Back for dinner at six after a good day's work, he ate leisurely, talking with mother and the children about the happenings of the day and joining in with our jokes and guessing riddles. Dinner over, he spent a half hour idly over his coffee and then his rest period was done. He retired at once to his study and stayed until long after we children were in bed. Twelve to thirteen hours of hard, confining work each day, but it seemed to agree with him...*

He never drank any liquor, and he spent no time in idle talk with companions. He never smoked, and neither drinking nor smoking were permitted in his house. He rarely visited others and very few visited him, because, I think, they realized that they were not welcome unless they came for a serious purpose and left when their errand was accomplished…He never played cards or other games except an occasional game of checkers with one of his sons, which he always won.

Everywhere, Clarence Burton's life grew. His business grew: in 1891, he bought out the other partners at his law firm and organized the Burton Abstract and Title Company. He and Harriet had three more children. In 1892, he added a new wing to the house and hired a secretary to accommodate his books.

"It would seem now that he had room enough for any man's books," Frank Burton wrote, "but day by day boxes of books and manuscripts arrived, some from local sources, others from the East or from London." A few years later, Burton built an addition to the addition to keep pace with his stuff.

Burton scoured rare book auction catalogues, corresponded with collections all over the world and trawled for the missing pieces of history that would fill in the gaps in his library. He found the papers of John Askin—a British merchant who came to Detroit in the 1760s—in an abandoned chicken coop and rode home sitting on top of them in the back of a horse cart. When he learned about a document with Antoine de la Mothe Cadillac's signature on it, he signed a blank check and sent it to Montreal. He tracked down and interviewed elderly Detroiters, old-time residents and relatives of famous citizens, sometimes asking whether they had any musty old trunks of family papers in their cellars, attics or sheds.

He traveled when he could. In 1898, he made a cross-country trek "in the footsteps of Cadillac"—his singular biographical obsession— from Quebec City and Montreal to Bar Harbor and Nova Scotia. In 1904, he re-created a portion of Cadillac's voyage on the French River in authentic birch-bark canoes. (Reportedly, Burton was not well suited to eating out of tins and sleeping on the ground.) And in 1907, he finally visited France as part of a grand tour of Europe, western Asia and North Africa. At St. Nicolas de la Grave—Cadillac's reputed birthplace—the local archaeological society regaled Burton with tales from its sleepy medieval past.

When he couldn't travel, he sent away for documents (such as the St. Nicolas de la Grave parish records) and had them transcribed and translated.

Personal tragedy only made him burrow deeper into the past. His wife, Harriet, died suddenly in 1896, leaving him to raise eight children alone. He remarried in 1897, but his second wife, Lina Shoemaker Grant, died less than a year later after contracting an infection during routine surgery. (This sad streak ended when he married his cousin, Anne Monroe Knox, in 1900. She brought four children from a previous marriage into the family, and they had one more child together.)

In 1913, Burton built a new house in Boston-Edison, leaving the Brainard Street house—and the colossal library inside of it—to the Detroit Public Library. Over the course of forty years, Burton had amassed thirty thousand books, forty thousand pamphlets and fifty thousand unpublished papers relating to Detroit, the Michigan Territory, the old Northwest, Canada and New France.

He continued to visit his library every day to research books, papers and presentations for the Michigan Pioneer and Historical Society, the Detroit Historical Society and the Michigan Historical Commission, all of which he chaired at some point. In 1922, he published his definitive multi-volume text, *The City of Detroit, 1701–1922*.

His masterwork, however, remains the Burton Collection, which was moved to the main branch of the Detroit Public Library on Woodward Avenue in 1921. The library sold Burton's house on Brainard back to him; the library used the money to start an endowment fund for his collection.

The Burton Historical Collection is still at the main branch today, in a midcentury modern room built as part of the library's 1963 addition. You still have to search by card catalogue. From the belly of the storage floors, archivists muster up two-hundred-year-old newspapers, boxes of letters in impeccable script, creaky scrapbooks and folders full of photographs.

Above it all, a portrait of Clarence Burton presides: mustachioed, wide-eyed, his aspect dead-serious. And while I'm not sure whether he would appreciate how much giggling I do there, I still say a silent "thank you" every time I visit.

THE GENERAL

I don't remember how or when, exactly, I ran into General Friend Palmer for the first time, but my acquaintance with him and his city has been one of my most cherished.

I probably picked up his book, *Early Days in Detroit,* as an amusement—reminiscences of French damsels, horse carts, beaver hats and voyageurs, sketched vividly between passages about who married whom, which forgotten territorial soldier lived at what address or which general store burned down when. And my goodness—those rotten Indians and their barbarous ways.

It is a deeply imperfect history, and for at least one good reason: Palmer died the day before his appointment with his editors. Since *Early Days* is a book of recollections, they didn't feel quite right making any

General Friend Palmer at the offices of the *Detroit Free Press. Burton Historical Collection, Detroit Public Library.*

changes without his say-so. Thus, "with a tender appreciation of Friend Palmer's loveable and kindly characteristics, we present this book in its present crude but authentic form," wrote his editors H.P. Hunt and C.M. June in 1906.

Some of the essays were written for newspapers and republished. Some were abridged versions of works submitted to the Pioneer Society or other historical digests. Other sections may have been written specifically for *Early Days*. So the book—over a thousand pages of it—is intact and unencumbered by shackles of chronology, narrative arc or consistent factual information.

It sounds like a disaster, perhaps not worth its real estate on the bookshelf. But what Palmer misses in his often wrong dates and sometimes repeated anecdotes, he more than makes up for in charm, wit and raw storytelling gusto. There are plenty of resources you can consult if you're looking for names, dates and facts. But who else can give you memories of shopkeeper Peter Desnoyers, blue-eyed and hilarious, selling goose yokes to the bratty neighborhood kids? Or personal memories of Father Gabriel Richard's sermons at St. Anne Catholic Church? Or casual accounts of stray, stubborn donkeys like this one:

> *The wide commons in the rear of the capitol were, during the summer months, covered in many places with a dense growth of weeds that grew almost as high as one's head. On this common and through these weeds the horses and cattle roamed at will, and among them was a stubborn donkey, the property of Colonel D.C. McKinstry. This donkey was an especial pet of the boys, and many tried to ride him. He would allow them to get on his back and get comfortably seated; then he would start off at a canter, with a loud bray, up would go his heels and over his head would go the boy.*

The Burton Collection is home to the general's stiff, crumbly scrapbooks—a couple dozen of them. (Burton and the general were contemporaries; *Early Days* includes some corrections by Burton to Palmer's historical articles. Palmer even writes once, on the topic of how Michigan came to be known as the Wolverine State: "I do not know for a certainty, but Clarence Burton does.")

Inside the scrapbooks is a bright, funny and darling cross-section of the general's delights: a page spread of articles about Napoleon; recipes for including more onions—nature's health and longevity miracle—in your diet; tips for being a better husband and quotes about families that suggest Palmer's affection for his own spouse, Harriet, and their children; and another page spread of foxy Victorian ladies suggesting that the general was also, well, a man.

Palmer was born in Canandaigua, New York, in 1820. He came to Detroit in 1827 with his mother—two days and two nights on a stagecoach from Canandaigua to Buffalo and then from Buffalo to Detroit across Lake Erie on the steamer *Henry Clay*. His father, also named Friend, had arrived three months earlier on urgent business for his chain of general stores, F&T Palmer, which he co-owned with his brother Thomas (with locations at Detroit, Canandaigua and Ashtabula, Ohio).

Tragically, the Palmer family would not be together for long; less than a month later, Friend Palmer Sr. died of pneumonia, which the younger Friend supposed he might have contracted after clearing his cellar of two feet of water in anticipation of the family's arrival. "I was too young to realize our loss," the general wrote.

In the winter of 1842, when Palmer was twenty-two years old, he left Detroit for Buffalo to work at a bookstore, where the owners also happened to be agents for the express service firm Pomeroy and Company—an early incarnation of American Express.

"It…necessitated my sleeping at the store," he wrote, "as the express manager came in at midnight and I had to be on hand to receive him and take charge of the money packages, etc. For fear something might happen when the messenger and porter routed me out, the company provided me with a revolver, a six-shooter, the same as the messengers carried, a clumsy affair, though I never had occasion to use it."

In 1846, he left the business to serve in the Mexican-American War. After that war, Palmer stayed in the military. During the Civil War, he served as assistant quartermaster general for the state of Michigan, was promoted after the war and held the office of quartermaster general until 1871, when he retired to business pursuits, writing and clerking at bookstores.

Palmer's Detroit is in some ways unrecognizable. As a boy, he watched steamboats on the river and stood in the kingly presence of steamer captains like Walter Norton, who helmed the steamer that brought the general to Detroit:

> *A man of fine presence, and he used to cut a swell figure...clad in his blue coat, with its brass buttons; nankeen trousers, white vest, low shoes, white silk stockings, ruffled shirt, high hat, not forgetting the jingling watch chain and seals.*

As a young man, he danced at all-night winter parties and walked French damsels home through the snow. He drove rickety horse carts through swampy streets. Sometimes the lynchpins came loose, toppling all of the carts' passengers into the mud.

He lived through the mind-raking here-one-day, gone-the-next devastation wracked by two successive cholera outbreaks, the frightening and out-of-control grief of watching your friends, neighbors and prominent citizens hauled off in carts. After seeing a funny play at the theater, the general wrote:

> *The old sexton, Israel Noble, mounted on his horse and followed by half a dozen drays and carts, each one laden with dead bodies, warned us all to shut up the theatre and wait until a later day, when finally the cholera disappeared as suddenly and as strangely as it came.*

But as lost to time as that time is, there are moments of harmony—kindred glimpses—that obliterate the narrow thoroughfares between here and now. Like the passage in *Early Days* in which the general snoops around in a dilapidated graveyard, making friends with the dead and looking for stories. Or the shiver of familiarity in some old black-and-white postcards of Belle Isle pasted in his scrapbooks. The island park looks largely the same today as it did in Palmer's time, except for a few buildings repurposed or erased from the landscape. He must have pleasured there on hot summer afternoons, perhaps with Harriet and the girls. Maybe they took a buggy ride. He probably ran into friends.

Did the general ever sit at his desk, wondering forward into the future, where I sit on my front porch, or on the riverfront or at the library with a fragile scrapbook wondering back at him? When I find one of his notes in the margins of his scrapbooks—like the one where he crossed out an incorrect illustration that accompanied one of his articles and wrote, "No! this is Sheldon & Rood's boosktore!" or the one next to a clip about the inner workings of a printing press ("I visited once.")—it's hard not to think, "Did he leave these notes for me?"

Belisle: Nay; tell me, first. You speak of Le Pesant, who killed Pere del Halle and La Riviere. What know you of him?

Roy: Ha, ha, ha, my dear doctor and father confessor! I know—that he is an Indian.

De Mersac: And more?

Roy: Aye, more; I may marry his daughter.

De Tonty: If the commandant permits it.

Roy: O the commandant! Always the commandant! Hark you, captain: I was here before any of you. Shall I bow down to the son of an advocate as he were the king?

De Tonty: Beware, my fine falcon! There are bigger birds than you. And we are all vassals of Monsieur Cadillac here, whether we like it or no.

Belisle: Whether we like it or no. I have heard men say—draw closer, friends—I have heard men say they would they were back in France, and will desert as soon as may be.

Roy: Ha, ha! That is no secret; our little Grande Monarque himself knows that.

THE GRAND MONARQUE OF VILLE DE TROIT

Detroiters like to begin this story on July 24, 1701, on the rough, weedy banks of the Detroit River. With daylight on the water and the wilderness humming with bugs, birds and fruit so fat you can hear it hanging from its branches, a fleet of fifty canoes glides up to the edge of the land. Sometimes they let Antoine de la Mothe Cadillac, the expedition's leader, set the scene himself:

> It is in this land, so fertile, that the ambitious vine, which has never wept under the knife of the vine-dresser, builds a thick roof with its large leaves and heavy clusters, weighing down the top of the tree which receives it, and often stifling it with its embrace.
>
> Under these broad walks one sees assembled by hundreds the timid deer and faun, also the squirrel bounding in his eagerness to collect the apples and plums with which the earth is covered. Here the cautious turkey calls her numerous brood to gather the grapes, and here also their mates come to fill their large and gluttonous crops. Golden pheasants, the quail, the partridge, woodcock and numerous doves swarm in the woods and cover the country, which is dotted and broken with thickets and high forests of full-grown trees, forming a charming perspective, which sweetens the sad lonesomeness of the solitude. The hand of the pitiless reaper has never mown the luxurious grass upon which fatten woolly buffaloes, of magnificent size and proportion...

If the situation is agreeable, it is none the less important because it opens and closes the door of passage to the most distant nations which are situated upon the borders of the vast seas of sweet water. None but the enemies of truth could be enemies to this establishment so necessary to increase the glory of the king.

The men—some of them soldiers in uniforms, with brass buttons that blink in the sun, and some of them Canadian privateers who have been singing, swearing and chain-smoking for the past six weeks—select a bluff on the north face of the river, shore the boats and strike camp. Cadillac claims *la ville de troit*—"city on the straits"—for the glory of God and King Louis XIV.

It's a beautiful frontier yarn—brave, rugged and holy. As the trees begin to fall under the axes of the voyageurs, a sweeping tale of settlement, struggle, progress, politics, industry and identity begins. Before the brash wind of Chicago began to blow, before the steamship

Louis XIV delivering to Chevalier de Cadillac the ordinance and grant for the foundation of the city of Detroit. Fernand LeQuesne, 1902, from a print. *Burton Historical Collection, Detroit Public Library.*

settled the canal towns of Pittsburgh and Buffalo, before Moses Cleaveland settled his city in Ohio and even before this same French empire founded New Orleans, the continent had Detroit.

Just as easily, we could begin this tale at the court of Versailles, where Cadillac traveled in 1698 to present his proposal for a French colony at what would become Detroit. Of course, the Company of the Colonies already had a trading post at Michilimackinac, which Cadillac commanded, but our reliably grand protagonist envisioned something bigger: a permanent establishment, with permanent settlers—a perfectly civil French society living in harmony with, and improving the lives of, the local Indian tribes. The idea was radical, and it had its detractors—Cadillac never lacked detractors—but the opportunity to thwart English designs on the region and control a major byway of the economically crucial fur trade won over the chamber. A 1902 painting by Fernand LeQuesne commemorates the dramatic moment when the king granted Cadillac the deed to the colony, as well as fifteen acres therein to call his own. Cadillac bows, the king stands in his sun-like splendor, curly wig and pretty buckle shoes, and the court of Versailles ricochets with Manifest Destiny and fatal extravagance.

But to really start wrestling with the Cadillac mystique, perhaps we must begin this story in the rural town of St. Nicolas de la Grave, Gascony, where Antoine de la Mothe was born on March 5, 1658. His middle-class parents did not grant him the regal title *Sieur de Cadillac*, so inextricable from Detroit's history, so gracefully evocative of American automotive style: Antoine invented it for himself. We don't know much about his early life, except that he left for Canada in 1683, possibly under duress.

"This Cadillac," stated Louis-Alexandre Des Friches de Meneval, governor of Acadia, "who is the most uncooperative person in the world, is a scatter-brain who has been driven out of France for who knows what crimes."

Cadillac's career began in Nova Scotia, where he took up with the privateer Francois Guion, learned the lay of the coastal lands, fell in love with the boss's niece, Marie-Therese, married her in Quebec and returned, somehow, to a twenty-five-mile land grant on the island of Mont Desert. The rest of his time in Acadia was apparently spent arguing with the governor. This became a motif in Cadillac's career.

During what we will call the abridged years, the English burned down the town where Cadillac lived. Cadillac lost his house and everything else and returned for Quebec. I am not sure what happened to his landholdings, but we do know that Mont Desert, the highest point on the north Atlantic seaboard—and, in the winter, the first place in the United States to see the sun rise—is named Cadillac Mountain. Meneval couldn't say a single nice word about him, but the French empire saw something in the feisty upstart and sent him to Michilimackinac to take over as commandant in 1694. Though under his tenure the diplomatic affairs of the post were "extremely confused," he made a pretty penny in the fur trade, and as he accumulated wealth, his status as an influential asset to French power remained secure.

Just a few years later, the king declared the French fur markets saturated and withdrew all licenses from existing trading posts. The king invited Cadillac to stay. Cadillac didn't want to. He was a fortune-maker, not a military middle manager. He left for France. Maybe he hatched his master plan on the long sail.

And this is where the story comes back to where we started: the court of Versailles, the parade of canoes, the axes and the high, verdant bluff of the newest holding of New France. Cadillac got his city on the straits. It was the most triumphant moment of his career.

It did not take long for Cadillac to start annoying people. Before fall, at least one member of the party had had enough of the place—or its charges d'affaires. Possibly because of a tiff over seniority, possibly because he learned of Cadillac's plan to populate the settlement by encouraging his settlers to marry local Huron girls, Father Francois Vaillant, one of two Jesuit priests, turned heel and left for Mackinac. The disregard was mutual: Cadillac had already written to Montreal to complain about Father Vaillant.

In September 1702, Marie-Therese and Marianne de Tonty arrived after a trek through Iroquois territory. It was an unusual voyage for any woman to take, made even more unorthodox by the route they chose, through Lake Ontario and Lake Erie and north to Detroit instead of down the Ontario River and through Lake Huron to the south. It was rough, uncharted and dangerous. The arrival of the first European women in the settlement signified to the colony and everyone paying

The women of the Detroit Bicentenary committee dedicated this plaque to the memory of Marie-Therese Guillon, Madame de la Mothe Cadillac, to celebrate the bicentennial of her arrival in Detroit. *Carlos Romanelli, 1903. Photo by the author.*

attention in Montreal and Paris that Detroiters were here for the long haul. Marianne and Marie-Therese were busy right away taking care of matters previously neglected, like administrative affairs (hiring, firing and contracting) and healthcare (Marie-Therese single-handedly served as the colony's doctor).

Cadillac ran Detroit like a lordship. Land grants for farms were technically free, but you had to play Cadillac's game. If you wanted your grain ground to flour, you had to do it at his gristmill—and pay for the privilege. If you wanted to bake bread, you baked it in Cadillac's oven. He charged fees for rent, trading rights and livestock. Licenses for artisan skills—brewing, for example—often required you to pay Cadillac in trade (like free beer). There was only one horse in Detroit, and Cadillac owned it. If you needed a horse, you rented that one.

He sparred with the Company of the Colonies in Montreal (which controlled the fur trade), the governor in France and the Jesuits at home, whom, he whined, he could please in only three ways: "The first is to let them do as they like; the second is to do everything they wish; the third to say nothing about what they do."

Grousing locals, a grudge-holding governor, disaffected Indians, conspiring priests and, to top it all off, a disappointing economic progress report for Detroit that fell far short of Cadillac's incessant hype—by 1710, the jig was up. King Louis abruptly terminated Cadillac's appointment and ordered him to proceed directly to Louisiana, where he would become governor.

But Cadillac did not proceed directly to Louisiana. In fact, after a brief stop in Quebec—where he submitted desperate (and ultimately failed) claims to property in Detroit that stretched from Lake Erie to Lake Huron and west from the river for some seven hundred miles—he went back to France. When he returned to the colony in Louisiana, he brought a boatload of eligible French girls for colonists to wed. It is not clear whether they improved the mired morale of the swampy southern colony.

Cadillac hated Louisiana and wrote volumes of correspondence to various ministers and bureaucrats in France airing his grievances. (Let's be fair: he may have been a little disgruntled about losing all of his property in Detroit.) In one letter, he described the residents of the colony as "the refuse of Canada," insisted that Louisiana was "not worth a straw" and declared the entire continent "not worth having." The colonists, he said, wanted to run away. In another, he simply wrote: "Bad country; bad people."

Louisiana didn't like Cadillac very much, either, and in 1716, Cadillac was released from his post. Upon his return to France, Cadillac continued to bad-mouth Louisiana until he was thrown in the Bastille for a few months to cool down.

So, what became of Detroit's founding father—the entrepreneur, profiteer, opportunist, explorer, quarreler and self-styled marquis? When last we meet our protagonist, he is trying—one last time—to restore his land and regain his power in Detroit. His claims are denied, but the council that reviews them throws him some bones: a few buildings, a few arpents of land, some cattle.

He does not pursue these properties. Instead, he retires to a small-town governorship in Castlesarrasin, just over the river from his hometown, St.

Nicolas, and lives the last years of his life in relative obscurity. Cadillac dies in 1730 at age seventy-two.

More than two hundred years later, the Detroit Historical Society gave the town of St. Nicolas de la Grave $20,000 to refurbish a home in the village—the home in which he was allegedly born—as a *Musée de Cadillac*. Four thousand miles from the state of Michigan stands a distinctive green-and-gold Michigan historical marker, flagging the spot where the story of Detroit began. Or did it?

"It has been attempted to fix the St. Nicholas de la Grave, in the south of France, as his birthplace, but, at the present time, I am unwilling to concede that he was born at this place," Clarence M. Burton wrote in *A Sketch of the Life of Antoine Cadillac*, the monograph he published in 1895. Burton searched St. Nicolas de la Grave parish records and found inconclusive evidence. An Antoine Laumet was born on December 4, 1653—which would make Cadillac a shade older than most of his other records indicate—but Burton wasn't convinced that Antoine Laumet and Antoine de la Mothe were one and the same.

Other researchers were. When Burton visited France in 1907, he found a memorial tablet mounted on the side of a tiny house proclaiming it Cadillac's birthplace; the street it faced had been recently and ceremoniously renamed "Rue de Cadillac."

Burton just went with it. In an essay recounting a charming visit to the home and the local archaeological society, he added a sly footnote regarding Cadillac's lineage, parentage and personal history: "There is something uncertain, and possibly undetermined, about the name and antecedents, but we will pass over that for the present, hoping that the story will be untangled in the future."

By then, the Carmelite convent where Cadillac was entombed in an unmarked vault had been converted to a prison. Plans brewed between Burton and some rich former Detroiters to bring Cadillac's bones and his tiny, ancient house—brick by brick and with a few bags of the earth beneath it for good measure—back to Detroit for a proper interment and memorial. It never happened.

A century later, the *Detroit Free Press* sent a reporter to France to check up on the Cadillac legacy in Gascony. When Gerry Volgenau asked leading French Cadillac researcher Jean Boutonnet whether the *Musée de Cadillac* could actually be Antoine's birthplace, Boutonnet simply said, "Impossible."

Some uncertainty, however, is entirely appropriate for someone of whom Catholic historian Jean Delanglez once said: "No statement by Cadillac is ever to be accepted unless corroborated by independent evidence…[Where] his interests are at stake, almost every statement of his which can be checked has turned out to be inaccurate, misleading or totally false."

Antoine Cadillac: more than three hundred years later, you're still keeping us guessing.

TRAVELING WITH LEWIS CASS

When you traveled with Governor Lewis Cass, you traveled in style, wrote C.C. Trowbridge, who was on the 1820 expedition to the headwaters of the Mississippi River.

"The General always carried a well-selected though necessarily a small library, and in his own canoe, when the weather permitted, some young member of the party was called upon to read aloud during a part of the forenoon.

Some might think this a monotonous way of traveling, and no doubt it would be so now, when anything less than five hundred miles in twenty-four hours is called a waste of time; but it was not so. The chanson de voyage in setting out in the morning and approaching the camp ground in the evening, under the graceful folds of our national flag, the bustle of pitching tents, cooking supper, fighting mosquitoes, gumming the canoes, and the long stories of adventure told by one of the old voyageurs…made the time pass cheerily…As to the evening camp fire proper of General Cass, it was always enlivened by some literary or scientific discussion, generally started by the general, and carried on by some of the savans in his suite."

STRANGERS

At the inaugural meeting of the Historical Society of Michigan in 1828, Territorial Governor Lewis Cass, the society's first president, gave the keynote address. Of Detroit, he said in his speech:

Five times its flag has changed, three different sovereignties have claimed its allegiance, and since it has been held by the United States, its government has been thrice transferred; twice it has been besieged by the Indians, once captured in war, and once burned to the ground. Identified as we are with its future fate, we may indulge the hope that its chapter of accidents has closed and that its advancement will be hereafter uninterrupted.

The historical society's founders were all Detroiters, and each a luminary—along with Cass, they included explorer, geologist, writer and Indian agent Henry Rowe Schoolcraft, who discovered the source of the Mississippi River in 1832; C.C. Trowbridge, merchant, ethnologist and later mayor of Detroit; Zina Pitcher, a military surgeon and future president of the American Medical Association, who also served as mayor of Detroit; and Father Gabriel Richard, pioneer priest, educator and tireless advocate of the poor, the sick and the illiterate, as well as the preservation of the Union.

What did these people even talk about at the first meeting of the Historical Society of Michigan? They *were* the history of Michigan.

TRIAL BY FIRE

Sulpician priest Gabriel Richard sailed from France to the United States in 1792 on *La Reine des Couers*. He was twenty-five years old, Jacobins were persecuting members of the clergy and he was casting himself into exile. Eight months later, the bishop of Saintes, Richard's hometown, was guillotined.

Sulpicians first took sanctuary in Baltimore, founding St. Mary's Seminary in an old tavern on the edge of town. As more members of France's persecuted Catholic clergy arrived, the diocese sent them farther afield, to minister to settlements throughout New England and western outposts in present-day Ohio, Illinois, Michigan and Missouri. Baltimore's bishop sent Richard to Kaskaskia, near St. Louis, where the young priest perfected his English, preached to his unruly and often drunken parishioners, learned to canoe like a champ and otherwise adjusted to the rigors of American frontier life.

In 1798, Richard was transferred to Detroit, where he became part of the scenery. You have to wonder whether Richard felt especially at home in Detroit, which for nearly a century had remained distinctively French in culture and character. Still, there was no one in Detroit like Gabriel Richard—tall, gaunt, bespectacled and dressed at all times in black cassock, wooden shoes and a shovel hat. He had a prominent scar on his face—some gossiped that it was from a sword fight with a Jacobin. There's little romance and not an ounce of politics in what actually happened: An unremarkable and unfocused student at seminary, Richard was horsing around on some chapel scaffolding when he fell and cracked his jaw.

June 11, 1805, ushered in a rough decade or so for Detroit. That afternoon, a baker went to the mill for some flour. While tying up his pony cart (for some reason, the pony always figures prominently in this story), he knocked some ash from his pipe, which a gust of wind blew into a pile of hay through the open door of a barn. The hay went up in a blaze, and the barn with it, and the famous pony—still hitched to the cart—bolted down the avenue. In a few hours, Detroit—a cramped and narrow town built from old wood—burned to the ground.

For the second time in its history, Ste. Anne was destroyed. The church, established by Antoine de la Mothe Cadillac one day after his arrival in

Detroit, first burned down in 1714. (The congregation went without a permanent home until 1755.)

But Richard was not concerned, for the moment, with his church. While the flames raged, Richard recruited a relief effort, organizing French farmers into canoe teams that crawled up and down the river, gathering eggs, flour, milk and other staples to feed the devastated community.

After the fire subsided, as Detroiters strung up bowers on the common, Richard jury-rigged an altar in an orchard and held services in the open air.

TRIAL BY WAR

It is hard to imagine portly, droopy-faced Lewis Cass as a young man, but so he was in 1811. Eleven years earlier, the Exeter graduate and New Hampshire native had come to Marietta, Ohio—seat of the Northwest Territory—with his father. He started a law practice, got married and began to build a life on the frontier. He was twenty-nine years old and doing well for himself.

Cass was a member of the Ohio Militia. When he heard that General William Henry Harrison, governor of the Indiana Territory, was marching into Shawnee Territory to take on Tecumseh, Cass knew that something big was about to go down. He closed his law office, mustered his volunteers and marched to Dayton to await further instructions.

It's hard to sum up the wonky war between Britain, the United States and a loose Indian confederacy in much less than a book, and I'm not going to try. It's safe to say, however, that a key component of the War of 1812 was Britain's attempt to retake the Northwest—and there is no Northwest without Detroit.

Detroit's importance to national security and prosperity predates the automobile by a heavy century. And the war was an early proving ground for people who would come to steer the city's fortunes for the rest of the nineteenth century—people like Lewis Cass.

Cass and his volunteers were placed under the command of William Hull, a reluctant fifty-eight-year-old veteran of the American Revolution

The Honorable Lewis
Cass of Michigan,
circa 1855–65. *Library
of Congress, Prints &
Photographs Division, LC-
DIG-cwpbh-02843.*

and governor of the Michigan Territory. Cass spent most of the War of
1812 playing frustrated second fiddle to the "Old Lady," as Hull's troops
called him.

When Hull carelessly placed some sensitive papers aboard the schooner
Cuyahoga—which was promptly seized by the British—Hull dispatched
Cass to the British fort at Malden to politely request their return. (The
British said, "No, but thanks.")

Hull sent Cass on recon to plan President James Madison's proposed
invasion of Canada. Friendly French-Canadians welcomed the American
troops warmly, and Cass took the village of Sandwich, in Ontario, without
a fight. Outnumbered British soldiers began to pack up Fort Malden
and evacuate. A few days later, Cass seized an important bridge over
the Canard River, clearing a four-mile straight shot to the fort. Still, the
ulcerative Hull hemmed and hawed. When he refused to call an advance,
Cass had to march his troops back to Sandwich, where Hull sat boarded
up in a mansion, seized by paranoia and dread. Cass was hailed as the

"Hero of the Tarontee." Hull was sowing mutiny. And what happened next was a humiliation so great, Detroit has only recently lived it down.

On August 13, 1812, Lieutenant Isaac Brock marched toward Malden with reinforcements, and Hull began to get a bad feeling about the number of Indians that he assumed were joining them. Brock knew that Hull was frightened and that his soldiers were feeling demoralized. He decided that he could seize Fort Detroit immediately.

Days before the fateful surrender of Detroit, Hull sent Cass into the country along a rotten overland bridle path to clear his communication route and meet a rendezvous that never showed up.

Rumors persist to this day: Did Cass know that Hull was planning to surrender Detroit? Did Hull know that Cass would try to stop him—maybe through a course as extreme as a mutiny or a coup?

There is a story Detroiters sometimes tell, that Major General Charles Larned circulated a document signed by eighty men—including Cass—declaring their intent to seize and depose Hull, leave Cass in charge and fight to keep Detroit. But like Cass, those who had signed the declaration were deposed on errands and absent during the siege. Whether this was an actual case of thwarted mutiny or a retroactive justification for the loathing and powerlessness so many of those fighters felt is unclear.

On the night of August 15, Brock began to bombard the fort, hoping to force the Americans into a fight. Tecumseh's force of Indian warriors had rowed across the river in the middle of the night and were paraded through the forest, raising loud war whoops, trying to create the illusion that there were thousands of them.

Hull must not have realized that his forces outnumbered the British and their allied Indian warriors by nearly two to one—in part because of Brock's canny bluffs, such as having his soldiers go through the mess line at meal time over and over again to give the appearance, across the river, of an army three times its actual size. Besides, many civilian Detroiters—the elderly, women and children, including Hull's daughter and young grandchild—lived within the stockade, and Hull feared a bloodbath like the one the fort had seen in 1763 during Chief Pontiac's rebellion. When the Americans began to incur casualties from British guns, Hull, in his office, quietly drafted a formal surrender and sent out his son, Captain Abraham Hull, to wave the white flag at advancing British troops.

On August 16, 1812—just sixteen years after the British evacuated under the terms of the Jay Treaty—Detroit fell under the British flag once again. It stayed there for nine months, until Oliver Hazard Perry's victory at the Battle of Lake Erie returned control of the Great Lakes and the Detroit River to the Americans.

For cowardice and treason, Hull was tried by court-martial and sentenced to death. President Madison commuted his sentence to dismissal from the army, which may have been what Hull wanted all along.

For his service in Detroit during 1812—and his commendable performance during the war, at the siege of Fort Meigs and at the Battle of the Thames, where Tecumseh was killed—Madison appointed Cass governor of the territory in 1813. He came to Detroit, a war-ravaged community in total disarray, to take control of a territory with hazy boundaries, few incentives for settlement and only four thousand permanent residents.

Cass was thirty-three years old.

EMPIRE BUILDERS

Father Gabriel Richard is frequently credited for every last inch of cultural growth in Detroit during the first two decades of the 1800s. Many of those claims are exaggerated—there is little evidence, for example, that Richard wrote and edited the entire first (and only) issue of the *Michigan Essay*, the first newspaper published in the Michigan Territory. But Richard *did* bring a printing press to Detroit in 1808, and it *was* the first that was used to print anything other than business forms, and it *did* print the *Essay*. He shipped the first harpsichords, spinning wheels and pipe organ into town. He recruited a sisterhood of well-bred, educated young women to run Detroit's first public schools. And with Augustus Woodward and Reverend John Montieth, he designed a college at Detroit that would later become the University of Michigan.

Richard was a powerhouse. Wrote his contemporary, Bishop Plessis of Quebec:

This grave-looking statue of Gabriel Richard used to stand at Old City Hall. Today it is on the grounds of Wayne State University. Sculpture by Julius Melchers, 1874. *Photo by the author.*

He has the talent of doing, almost simultaneously, ten entirely different things. Provided with newspapers, well informed on all political matters, ever ready to argue on religion when the occasion presents itself, and thoroughly learned in theology, he reaps his hay, gathers the fruits of his garden, manages a fishery fronting his lot, teaches mathematics to one young man, reading to another, devotes his time to mental prayer, establishes a printing press, confesses all his people, imports carding and spinning-wheels and looms to teach the women of his parish how to work, leaves not a single act of his parochial register unwritten, mounts an electrical machine, goes on sick calls at a very great distance, writes letters and receives others from all parts, preaches every Sunday and holy day both lengthily and learnedly, enriches his library, spends whole nights without sleep, walks for whole days, loves to converse, receives company, teaches catechism to his young parishioners, supports a girls school under the management of a few female teachers of his own choosing whom he directs like a religious community, while he gives lessons in plain song to young boys assembled in a school he had founded, leads a most frugal life, and is in good health, as fresh and able at the age of fifty as one usually is at thirty.

Wrote General Friend Palmer:

It was said that Father Richard was so studious and patient in his search after knowledge that he actually counted the eggs in a whitefish. How many millions, history fails to tell.

Richard is especially remembered as an advocate for public education. He wanted schools for boys, girls, poor children, children of means, Indian children, French children and the children of New Englanders. No organized public schools had existed before Richard's arrival in Detroit. By 1804, he had established a ladies academy and a school for boys. Both were destroyed during the fire.

In 1808, he wrote to the territorial judges:

Besides the English Schools in the Town of Detroit there are four primary schools for boys, and two for our young ladies…At Spring Hill, under the direction of Angelique Campau and Elizabeth Lyons, as early as the 9th of September last, the number of the scholars had been augmented by four young Indians, headed by an old matron, their grandmother, of the Pottowattamie tribe. In Detroit, in the house lately the property of Captain Elliott…there are better than thirty young girls who are taught…reading, writing, arithmetic, knitting, sewing, spinning, etc.

Richard also envisioned, though never fully achieved, a vocational school for Indian children that would teach them reading, writing, philosophy, geography, fine arts and math, as well as agriculture, mechanic trades, animal husbandry and household arts. The land grant he requested from President Thomas Jefferson was to include small plots for each family on which they could practice stewardship of their farms and lands.

Jefferson admired the idea but left office before he could give Richard what he needed: land and money. The project was tabled during President James Madison's administration and shelved during the War of 1812.

Back at the governor's office, Lewis Cass had one priority for his administration: attracting people to the territory.

A poorly conducted 1815 survey of the Michigan Territory reported most of the lower peninsula to be "interminable swamps," with one useful acre in a hundred at best. Cass called for a do-over.

The Cass expedition of 1820 went a step further. What if the territory was not only comfortably inhabitable but also profitable? Could the river or the upper lakes contain copper, iron, silver or other precious ores? He personally set out with a survey team, canoeing up and around the mitten of Michigan, north to Mackinac and the Upper Peninsula, west across the southern shore of Lake Superior and down the Mississippi. Cass and his party smoked peace pipes with tribal leaders across the region, hunted buffalo and beheld the huge copper rock on the Ontonagon River.

It made for rollicking reading, and accounts of the adventure were widely published, no doubt stirring many a stagnant New England imagination. The Cass expedition also produced a survey of the westernmost lands of the territory, later used to make maps that encouraged settlers to venture into the wilds. Cass put internal improvements at the top of the agenda and started building roads across the unsettled expanse.

The other component of Cass's plan for population growth was the acquisition of vast tracts of Indian lands in Michigan. In 1819, Cass negotiated the Treaty of Saginaw with Ojibwe chiefs Wosso and John Okemos. It gave the United States 6 million acres—most of the eastern portion of the lower peninsula—for $3,000 up front and $1,000 annually. (Cass had originally come to the council table hoping to remove the tribes to west of the Mississippi. He dropped it during negotiations.)

Emigrants from the Northeast—encouraged by new land for the grabbing and bolstered by advances in transportation, such as the steamboat and the Erie Canal—began to flow steadily into Michigan.

Richard saw education as the only way for poor French farmers to have a say in the society that was beginning to take shape. An ad published in the *Detroit Gazette* in August 1817—probably by Richard—pleaded:

> *Frenchmen of the Territory of Michigan! You ought to begin immediately to give an education to your children. In a little time there will be in the Territory as many Yankees as French, and if you do not have your children educated, the situations will all be given to the Yankees.*

The Yankees, for their part—contemporaries of Cass, the kind of "great men" who would come to lead, and define, the city in the next century—found the French habitants "exceedingly ignorant and lazy," in the words of Solomon Sibley. The French were not industrious people, complained the New Englanders—including Cass himself. They relied on the fur trade and the nice clothes, plentiful brandy and profligate downtime that came with it. If they wanted fish for dinner, they strolled down to the river and caught some. If they felt like fruit for dessert, they wandered back into their orchards and picked some. Territorial Judge Frederick Bates wished that he could do better with French girls. The habitants distrusted and disliked the Americans who were flooding their city. *Sacre cochon de Bostonnais*, they grumbled under their breath—Yankee pigs.

WASHINGTON

In 1823, pressured by his congregation, which wanted to see a Frenchman on the ballot, Gabriel Richard decided to run for Congress. His rival, John R. Williams—nephew of Joseph Campau, the richest man in Michigan—was outraged. He thought he had already secured the French Catholic vote, and besides, what place was there in Congress for this quirky old priest, with his broken English and goofy clothes? Williams took the Richard candidacy to task. Richard wasn't allowed to run for office, he alleged—he wasn't a citizen. And it was true.

Not to be daunted, Richard immediately applied for U.S. citizenship. A county court judge—who happened to be the campaign manager of a third candidate, Austin Wing—tried to turn Richard away, but the two other judges on the bench overruled him, and Richard was granted citizenship on June 28, 1823. With papers in hand—and a French citizenry infuriated over what they saw as blatant discrimination—Richard cruised to victory. He was the first priest in Congress. Williams and Campau left the Catholic church in disgust.

In 1831, Lewis Cass resigned as territorial governor to join President Andrew Jackson's cabinet as secretary of war, where he applied the expertise he had honed in Michigan toward Jackson's plans for Indian removal. Later in his career, after a term in the Senate, Cass ran for president against Zachary Taylor in 1848. But his conciliatory views on slavery—in particular his support for the Doctrine of Popular Sovereignty, which held that the residents of a territory, and not the federal government, should decide whether they would allow slavery—split his support within the Democratic Party.

During the cholera outbreak of 1832, Richard died at age sixty-five after tireless ministry and care for the sick. Whether he caught the disease or simply exhausted himself is unclear. Attendance at his funeral exceeded the total population of Detroit.

Richard and Cass had worked together and admired each other, but in some ways they represent competing interests and narratives of the city.

Cass's legacy is complicated, to say the least. He was the primary dealer in treaties that largely cleared Michigan of its native landholders and turned over their commonly held ancestral properties to private interests and prospecting. He sought compromise and moderation above all on the political question of slavery. But in moral hindsight—and compared with firebrands such as Detroit mayor, U.S. senator and unwavering abolitionist Zachariah Chandler, who helped found the Michigan Republican Party—compromise seems like its own insidious evil.

But there is no doubt that Cass played a major role in expanding Michigan's prosperity and national clout. Detroit's population nearly doubled during Cass's term as governor. By the time Cass died in 1866, Detroit's population exceeded fifty thousand. Under his administration, Detroit established a Common Council. He helped map Michigan's boundaries, identify its natural resources, set its legislative precedents and build its roads. There's a reason why a statue of Cass still stands on behalf of Michigan at the U.S. Capitol. (Chandler's, on the other hand, was removed in 2011 and replaced with a statue of President Gerald R. Ford.)

As for Richard, we too often forget, when we remember the universal good he did, that his life's work was a little subversive. As Cass filled his territorial government with *Bostonnais*, Richard tried his damndest to make sure that all Detroiters—those who couldn't read, didn't speak English or lacked the skills to work in the large-scale agricultural economy he saw coming—would be able to get an education and participate in their democracy. His legacy, prescient and perennially relevant, is brandished on the city. It is the declaration he is said to have made as he surveyed a charred and broken village the morning after the Great Fire of 1805: *speramus meliora, resurget cineribus*—we hope for better things; it shall rise from the ashes.

ONE CONSTANT SUCCESSION
OF AMUSEMENTS

D etroit, a century-old city by 1801, still seemed to some observers to be mired in its own provincial past. The single-industry river town was blessed with fertile soil, fair weather and an abundantly profitable fur trade.

With such an embarrassment of riches, who needed hard labor? French ladies did not spend time at the loom or the spinning wheel, nor did they bother much to improve the industry of their family farms. Writing to England in 1776, Detroit's British governor, Henry Hamilton, guessed that it was just *too easy* to live well in the settlement:

> *The backwardness in the improvement of farming has probably been owing to the easy and lazy method of procuring bare necessaries in this Settlement…The straight…is so plentifully stocked with a variety of fine fish that a few hours amusement may furnish several families, yet not one French family has got a seine…The soil is so good that great crops are raised by careless & very ignorant farmers…The great advantage to be drawn from the management of bees, has never induced any to try them here, tho there are wild bees in great numbers, and the woods are full of blossoming shrubs, wild flowers and aromatic herbs…The Inhabitants may thank the bounty full hand of Providence, for melons, peaches, plumbs, pears, apples, mulberries and grapes, besides several sorts of smaller fruits…grow wild in the woods.*

Forty years, two wars and three flag-raises later, newcomers still complained about how little the settlement had advanced. In 1816, Governor Lewis Cass complained to the secretary of war about Detroit's "defect of agricultural knowledge," describing with dismay (or disgust?) the farmers' lack of soap-making skills, their habit of throwing away wool and the winter tradition of dragging their manure into the frozen river "that it might be carried into the lake in the spring."

To hear it from the enterprising, Puritan-minded *Bostonnais*, the French *habitans*, though cheerful, were lazy and preferred to spend free time not on self-improvement, literary enrichment or devising some ingenious new method of beekeeping, but rather on drinking, dancing and flirting at the best parties in the old Northwest.

Detroit, however, was nowhere near, and nothing like, New England. Though it occupied a prime location at the gateway to the Great Lakes, that passage was useless for six icy months of the year. Detroit wasn't close to any other major city, and even if it were, there were no roads to get there. French farmers might not have used manure to fertilize or rotate their crops, but they clearly did okay for themselves, and what they didn't grow or raise themselves, they traded. French settlers had access to goods as refined as anything available in Montreal—even Philadelphia or New York.

Put simply, in the winter, there was nothing else to do. On Sundays, there was church, and then there was nothing else to do. Bring on the picnics, beach trips, boat trips, hunting outings, card games and races—on horse or on foot. ("The most celebrated racer is a Frenchman named [Louis] Campau; his superiority is so well recognized that he is no more admitted to the races," a visitor wrote in 1757.)

Of course, the humble, leisure-loving French farmer was not the only Detroiter who enjoyed a little fun here and there—parties were for everyone.

Late in his life, British commandant Arent Schuyler de Peyster's memory of Detroit gleamed. In a book of poems, *Miscellanies, by an Officer*, written after De Peyster's retirement, he commemorated (in clunky verse) a winter outing on the frozen Rouge River, where lords and ladies donned sable robes, grilled venison and drank Madeira. Even the wildlife was enraptured:

The goblet goes round, while sweet echo's repeating,
The words which have passed through fair lady's lips;
Wild deer (with projected long ears) leave off eating
And bears sit attentive, erect on their hips…

The fort gun proclaims when 'tis time for returning,
Our pacers all eager at home to be fed;
We leave all the fragments, and wood clove for burning,
For those who may drive up sweet River Red.
Freeze River Red, sweet serpentine river,
On you, carioling, be dear to me ever,
Where wit and good humor were ne'er known to sever
While drinking a glass to a croupe en grillade.

The early tradition of revelry rolled through the generations like amber clouds full of sparkling cider. As the nineteenth century grew fat with the promise of progress, Detroiters were still staying up all night dancing the money-musk. In his old age, General Friend Palmer fondly recalled the French parties of his youth:

Have any of you that read these lines ever been to a French dance given in a French farm house, not in a tavern? If you have, then you know all about it.

The large kitchen and living room, with its polished floor, quaint old-fashioned furniture, the tall clock in the corner, the huge cast-iron plate stove of two stories, brought in from Montreal in the early days, in which a scorching heat could be engendered in short order. "Music in the corner posted," which consisted of two violins. And then the gathered company, eager to begin, which they did always early in the afternoon, and kept it up until the small hours in the morning…

Money-musk, Virginia reel, Hunt-the-grey-fox, French four, the pillow dance and occasionally a cotillion. It did not seem to me as though the feet of the dancers would ever grow weary moving to the inspiring music of the French four, given on a violin, and as a Frenchman alone could give it.

The general noted that "refreshments" served in the "primitive style" were ample and then recounted the singular pleasure of walking your best girl home through the snow.

Not everyone was enchanted with the old ways. William Woodbridge, as secretary of the Michigan Territory, was obliged to spend many long, late nights making the social rounds, when he would no doubt rather have cozied up at home, reading philosophy books. Of life in Detroit, he wrote to his wife in 1815:

> *Of the society—what shall I tell you? One would think that the lives of this people consist in one constant succession of amusements—dances, rides, dinners, card parties, and all the et cetera of dissipation follow in one long train, treading each on the heels of the other.*

Twenty years later, Territorial Secretary John Thomson Mason wrote in a letter:

> *These fancy balls are a new introduction into our country and are the quintessence of the corruption of European society…It will add to no lady's reputation to say she has been at one.*

Unfortunately (or hilariously), Mason's children—Stevens T. Mason, the so-called Boy Governor of Michigan, and Emily Virginia Mason—were two of the most capable partiers in the territory.

At a soiree at the Hubbard House in Mt. Clemens in 1838—celebrating the groundbreaking of a canal that would link Lake St. Clair to Lake Michigan—Governor Mason was said to have knocked back fourteen toasts and then jumped up on the banquet table and paced back and forth. A commemorative article in 1938 (yes, the party was that good) shrugged off the governor's bad behavior: "Every adult male in Mt. Clemens was drunk that day."

But Detroiters hardly needed an excuse to pop a cork. Holidays? Notable visitors? Cold weather? The smallest resonance of historical occasion? All of it called for parades, pony races, costume balls, fireworks and dancing in the streets.

THE DETROIT HOLIDAY ALMANAC

New Year's Day

It was a long-held tradition in old Detroit. On January 1, society types made the rounds, calling on friends and neighbors and wishing good tidings for the year at hand. It was a sight that at least one resident found completely ridiculous. Wrote Joshua Toulmin Smith in his diary:

> *Folks here always go about calling on New Years day on* all *their friends—they go twos & twos or more & look most absurd—it happened to be a wet day this time & their Sunday best got sadly bespattered.*

The holiday, like most holidays, also called for eating and drinking to liver-crushing excess. In 1885, the competent but obnoxious lawyer Ebenezer Rogers helped himself to a New Year's Day banquet at Rice's Hotel. His "appetite was enormous and insatiable, and in addition to his regular meals [he] embraced every opportunity of filling his stomach with food that did not cost anything."

He died the next day, at seventy years of age, of "congestion of the stomach." In other words, he literally ate himself to death. It is unclear whether this is medically possible, but it seems appropriate.

Washington's Birthday

In a letter home in 1833, Julianna Woodbridge Backus dragged her father, that party-hating William Woodbridge, to a celebration of Washington's birthday. It was something to write home about, so she did:

> *The walls were festooned with pink, blue & white stars & stripes. There was a large black eagle & Washington's picture.*
>
> *I danced twelve times & once with the governor's son...There was not so many there as I expected, but we had more dancing. The great characters as mother calls them were Mrs. Porter with a great blue & white feather in her hair, the governor* [George Bryan Porter] *with*

"Norvell with great staring eyes… danced and drank until the tobacco ran out of his mouth." John Norvell, attributed to Thomas Sully. *Submitted to OTRS, via Wikimedia Commons.*

his whiskers that looked like a hedge. Norvell with his great staring eyes…danced & drank until the tobacco ran out of his mouth.

"Norvell" was John Norvell, a newspaper publisher and, at the time, postmaster general. He would become one of Michigan's first U.S. senators.

Mardi Gras

The French element in Detroit celebrated Mardi Gras with a pancake party, wrote Carrie Hamlin in 1883:

> *The tossing of pancakes (flannel cakes) or, as the French express it, virez le crepes, was an old custom handed down, and even to-day is still observed in my family. A large number of guests were invited to the house of one of the wealthier citizens, and all repaired to the spacious kitchen…Each guest would in turn take hold of the pan (la poele) with its long handle, while some one would pour in the thin batter, barely enough to cover the bottom of the pan. The art consisted of trying to turn the cake by tossing it as high as possible and bringing it down without injuring the perfection of the shape.*

May Day

It's spring, and that can mean only one thing: maypole dances. If you're lucky—okay, just if you're legally obligated to—you can even help raise the maypole at Antoine de la Mothe Cadillac's house, according to Clarence M. Burton:

> *In some [land] conveyances, there was a condition that the vendee should join others in setting up a May pole before the house of the commandant on the first of May in each year. Exemption from this condition could be purchased each year upon payment of three livres in money or skins.*

July Anniversaries

July is Detroit's month. The city celebrates the anniversary of its founding on July 23 or 24, depending on whether you count the night Cadillac and his party spent on Grosse Ile before backtracking the next day and planting the flag at present-day Hart Plaza.

If Detroiters (all 800 of them) celebrated their centennial anniversary in 1801, we don't have any record of it. But the bicentennial in 1901 (population: more than 300,000) was a blowout, complete with a reenactment of Cadillac's landing, military exercises, historical tableaux and pageants, the unveiling of several memorial tablets throughout the city, edifying lectures about Detroit's past (Silas Farmer spoke, as did Burton, who improvised a surprise lecture about Cadillac's life), automobile parades and a banquet at the Russell House for Monsieur and Madame Cadillac, where the band played "La Marseillaise." Representatives from France made Detroit mayor William Cotter Maybury an honorary chevalier of the Legion of Honor.

July 11 is Evacuation Day, celebrating the day in 1796 that the British left the Americans in control of Fort Detroit. On July 11, 1896, Mayor Hazen S. Pingree decked Detroit in red, white and blue bunting, and diplomats from across the country came to the city and celebrated with speeches, a parade, a "riotous waste of gunpowder" and lunch on a riverboat with a mandolin orchestra.

And of course, everyone loves the Fourth of July, a most reckless holiday. You could commemorate it the old-fashioned way, with a notable

Bicentennial celebration, floral clock and a Hiram Walker & Company float, Detroit, Michigan, 1901. *Library of Congress, Prints & Photographs Division, Detroit Publishing Company Collection, LC-D4-32546.*

citizen giving a public reading of the Declaration of Independence, or by drinking copious toasts on a steamboat cruise. Or you could light things on fire. Wrote General Friend Palmer of storekeepers John Owen and Captain John Edwards:

> *The then city marshal Adna Merritt [was] a nervous, excitable little body who used to get himself all tangled up trying to stop these two from starting and throwing fire balls, balls of cotton wicking soaked in turpentine and re-enforced with twine. It was quite common then on Fourth of July nights and on other nights as well, during the summer season, for the boys to ignite and throw these balls up and down Jefferson Avenue. Merritt tried to put a stop to it, but Owen and Captain Edwards were dead against his doing so and supplied all the fire balls necessary from Dr. Chapin's store. Did you ever see fire balls thrown or did you ever throw them yourself? 'Tis great fun, and attended with some danger to the hands, and some to*

property, although I never knew of any harm to come from them. After a short season both Owen and Edwards joined the Methodist church, having gotten religion. No more fire balls from that quarter after that.

Labor Day

The first Labor Day in the United States was celebrated in New York City in 1882. It caught on in no time. Here's an account from the Detroit chapter of the American Federation of Labor and Congress of Industrial Organizations:

Labor Day was celebrated here in a manner never before equalled. The press and public have showered praise upon us to an extent that would turn the heads of numbers of a less well-regulated organization than ours. We had 12,000 men and women in line. Nearly all the carriages in the city were preempted for the use of the ladies. Many prizes were given for well-appearing bodies and beautiful floats. The shoe workers got first prize for drill and general appearance, the machinery wood workers pulling down second; the caulkers union got first prize for a float upon which many of its members were occupied caulking the deck of a miniature boat, the second prize going to the garment workers, who had a very artistic float in rose, yellow and white…representing the goddess of justice with the scales in hand. It was a very significant emblem.

We have issued a souvenir of labor day. It will net clear of expenses $2,500, half of which goes in a fund for a labor temple to be erected, we hope, next year.

No record exists of such a labor temple ever coming to fruition.

Thanksgiving

Due in part to the influx of immigrants from New England, the first Thanksgiving in Detroit was officially celebrated on November 25, 1824, by decree of Governor Lewis Cass. The *Bostonnais* celebrated it more heartily than Christmas. You could even shoot your own turkey at the bar (more on that in the next chapter).

Christmas

Christmas was a social expression of Detroit's convergence of cultural forces. The many New Englanders living in Detroit introduced Christmas trees, the story of Santa Claus and "the pleasant custom of the interchange of presents." The Catholics held an "imposing" midnight mass at Ste. Anne Church. And on Christmas Eve, according to a German custom, everyone stayed up all night to make noise, according to Palmer:

> *It was quite the custom the night before Christmas to usher in the day with the blowing of horns and firing of guns, commencing at 12 o'clock and keeping it up until daylight...Woe betide the English-speaking or Protestant family who had a German girl for a domestic. Her admirers would commence at the appointed hour and keep it up till morn. The German maid would be in eager anticipation of the opening of the fusilade and grievously disappointed if it did not occur according to program.*

Let's face it: it wouldn't be a holiday in early Detroit without some reckless endangerment.

On Christmas Day, the stores were closed at noon, and the "horsey portion of the male community" came out for a French pony race on Jefferson Avenue (or right on the frozen river, if it wasn't snowy enough on the street). Indians who lived in nearby settlements would come downtown to join the party, and a local milliner would give them free festive hats.

At countryside homes, gigantic yule logs were hauled in from the woods and burned in the hearth, and Christmas dinners were served of "turkey, with the pumpkin and mince pies, white fish and always the new cider that had just commenced to sparkle."

A few nights later, on New Year's Eve, the calendar of parties returned to where it had started, and Detroit settled in for another festive year.

ENTERTAINMENT FOR ELECTION DAY

In 1792, David William Smith, commandant of Fort Niagara, ran for a seat in the provincial Parliament in Canada. In a letter to John Askin, he outlined entertainment to be provided for Detroit electors:

"The French people can easily walk…but my gentry will require some conveyance; if boats are necessary you can hire them and they must not want beef or rum, let them have plenty, and in case of success I leave it to you, which you think will be best to give my friends a public dinner, and the ladies a dance, either now, or when I go up. If you think the moment the best time you will throw open Forsyths Tavern, and call for the best he can supply. I trust you will feel very young on the occasion, in the dance, & I wish that Leith and you should push about the bottle, to the promotion of the Settlements on the Detroit. The more broken heads and bloody noses there is, the more election-like, and in case of success (damn that if!) let the white ribbon favors be plentifully distributed, to the old, the young, the gay, the lame, the cripple & the blind—half a score cord of wood piled hollow, with a tar barrel in the middle, on the Common, some powder… and plenty of rum."

LIQUOR

Here's a popular notion that is probably true: when Antoine de la
Mothe Cadillac set off from Montreal for Detroit in 1701, he
packed with his cargo fifteen barrels of brandy. Shortly after he arrived,
he ordered more—three hundred livres worth.

Some American towns were founded by religious pilgrims, some by
cranky homesteaders and others by new industries or favorable locations.
Detroit was founded by traders, and where you had trade, you had booze.

Cadillac also arrived with two Jesuit priests, which obviously caused
problems right away. Was it not wrong, the Jesuits begged, to introduce
the evils of alcohol to the local Indian community? Would it not promote
violence, crime and degradation?

In response to such concerns—borne out by what usually happened
when Europeans brought boatloads of brandy to town—the French
crown attempted to regulate the commerce of intoxicants. But it
couldn't outlaw it completely, traders argued, without killing trade, as
long as independent traders and the British had no problem trading
alcohol for pelts.

So Cadillac—in addition to his roles as commandant, trader-in-chief,
director of the bureau of land management and self-styled marquis du
Detroit (he asked King Louis for the title repeatedly)—became the city's
first liquor commissioner. From a central storehouse, he distributed his
eau de vie as rations for his soldiers—after all, no fish dinner was complete

without a little brandy—and as currency for Indian fur traders. And beer brewing was one of the many trades that Cadillac ruled could not be practiced without his say-so (along with blacksmithing, locksmithing and armor making). A couple of hogsheads of ale might even be part of your license fee.

For more than a century—under French rule, under British rule and as part of the United States—things went on like this in Detroit. People decried the trade of liquor, then participated in it despite its effects and then decried it some more.

After a visit to Mackinac in 1799, a despairing Father Gabriel Richard wrote:

> *The traders themselves confess that it would be better for their own profit not to give rum to the Indians, but as the Indians are very much fond of it, every trader says that he must give them rum not to lose all his trade…God knows how many evils will flow from that trade. Some have observed that English rum has destroyed more Indians than ever did the Spanish sword.*

Many historians have attributed Richard's public falling-out with the prominent trader Joseph Campau to Campau's liquor trade. Although they no doubt aggravated each other on the issue, Richard himself bought booze from Campau: large quantities of imported wine.

In 1798, Michigan held its first election in a bar. The race: the first representatives of the Michigan Territory to the U.S. Congress. The contenders: John May, a former British subject, and Solomon Sibley, an itinerant pioneer lawyer who came to Detroit by way of Ohio by way of New England. The setting: John Dodemead's home, tavern and sometimes county courthouse. After three days of voting, Sibley won the seat. John May accused him of plying voters with liquor to encourage their votes.

Dodemead was also the county coroner. After the official incorporation of Detroit in 1802, Dodemead was granted the city's first tavern license.

Sibley was active in city politics for the rest of his life. In 1815, he was chairman of the board that sought to create order in Detroit—standards and regulations that made it a real, functional city. Provisions included speed limits, a ban on horse racing, a fire code (violations: storing hay too close to a house, neglecting to keep your chimney clean and failure to keep two water buckets in your home), a one-dog limit per household and a twenty-dollar liquor license fee for taverns and places of public entertainment. Selling liquor on Sundays was against the law. "Drunken orgies in taverns" were punishable by fines from three to ten dollars.

In 1818, Benjamin Woodworth opened his new-and-improved hotel, renamed the Steamboat Hotel, just in time for the heralded arrival of the *Walk-in-the-Water*, the first steamboat to sail to Detroit from Buffalo, New York. Over the years, Woodworth's hotel had hosted many of Detroit's most important galas, including a Grand Pacification Ball celebrating peace between Britain and the United States after the Treaty of Ghent officially ended the War of 1812, as well as a reception for President James Monroe—the first president to visit Detroit—in 1817.

Woodworth shocked Detroit in 1830 when he offered to act as sheriff and hangman for Stephen Simmons, who was sentenced to death for killing his wife. Analysts blamed a drunken rage. It was the last state execution in Michigan's history.

By the mid-1830s, Detroit had one saloon for every 13 residents (total population: about 2,200). At a bar, you could get a free lunch, read any number of newspapers, smoke a cigar, play cards, discuss current affairs, conference with business associates, campaign and legislate. Visitor A.A. Parker wrote in 1835:

> *The streets near the water are dirty, generally having mean buildings, rather too many grog shops among them, and a good deal too much noise and dissipation. The taverns are not generally under the best regulations, although they were crowded to overflowing. I stopped at the Steamboat Hotel, and I thought enough grog was sold at that bar to satisfy any reasonable demand for the whole village.*

As Detroit's population exploded, so did its traffic in intoxicants. German immigrants in the 1840s—like Bernhard Stroh, whose family of innkeepers had brewed beer in Bohemia since the late 1770s—brought their refined lager style and genteel beer gardens to Detroit and planted an industry that would innovate, influence and prosper for the rest of the century.

Rack warehouse, Hiram Walker
& Sons, Walkerville, Ontario.
*Library of Congress, Prints &
Photographs Division, Detroit
Publishing Company Collection, LC-
D4-42672.*

Meanwhile, it was cheaper to make whiskey from grain than to ship it, so distilleries boomed. The city was so profligate with spirits that Detroit grocer and distiller Hiram Walker moved operations across the river, where real estate was cheaper, liquor laws were looser and competition was slight. From his Canadian distillery—in Walkerville, the town he founded, financed and settled himself—Walker produced the whiskey that became Canadian Club. Its international allure made it a top seller in America, annoying American distillers.

Bars for every taste, class and purpose sprang to life: bars for tourists and travelers, watering holes for local thirsts, bars with attached family restaurants where ladies were welcome (they weren't at most bars) and exclusive clubs for society types. At the Young American Saloon, opened in 1856, you could order meals "furnished at any hour, at a moment's notice."

The Bank Exchange bar published this little poem about its oysters:

> *Of all the oysters ever I see,*
> *At the Bank Exchange you will find the best.*
> *They come fresh right from the sea,*
> *And so are sold for less.*

The Bank Exchange also printed a guarantee that its seafood was better than its verse.

At Tom Dick's Barrel Bar, you had your choice of two brands of whiskey, served straight from a tapped wooden cask. The premium brand was best served neat. The other brand, "Twa Bits," was only remotely palatable when served with a couple lumps of sugar in the bottom of the glass—hence its name.

Seymour Finney, a tailor by trade, opened a tavern in 1850 and later a hotel in present-day Capitol Park. Next to the tavern he built a barn, where he sheltered escaped slaves traveling to freedom on the Underground Railroad. His customers at the bar, some of whom might have been slaveholders once, had no idea what was happening right behind them.

One of the oldest bars in town, known as the Old Shades (to distinguish it from the less old, but still really old, bar next door, the Shades), was creaky and moss-grown as early as the 1840s. When it was torn down in the 1880s, the *Detroit Free Press* declared the bar's history to be "lost to the gloom of antiquity." Its reporters were unable to find anyone alive—even the oldest of the old-timers—who could remember a time when the Shades was not an ancient place.

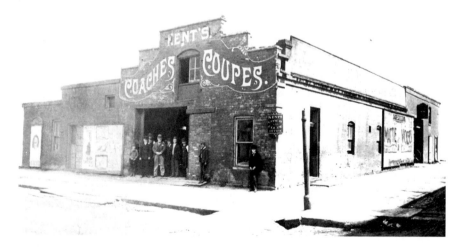

Seymour Finney kept a barn behind his inn and sheltered escaped slaves making their way to Canada along the Underground Railroad. *Ohio Historical Society.*

In the winter, when the river froze over, enterprising barkeeps would set up shanty saloons between Detroit and Canada. Traders hauling goods across the ice would stop for a drink or six, so trade traffic tended to take a steep dive during the cold months.

One bar on the rural outskirts of town offered a holiday attraction: shooting your own poultry. Wrote General Friend Palmer:

> *This tavern used to be well patronized by the farmers living near the city and by the general public. It was a grand place for shooting turkeys, geese and chickens Thanksgiving and Christmas. The fowls were securely fastened to a box or something some distance in the rear of the tavern…The crowd would load and fire from the back shed of the tavern, and when the day's fun was over, they would spend the night in the bar room raffling off the victims of the day.*

Temperance and Intemperance

In 1853, the Reverends J.A. Baughman and George Taylor unfurled a 1,300-foot-long bolt of cotton before the Michigan legislature. Pasted on the cloth were petitions in favor of a law prohibiting the sale of liquor except for medicinal, scientific and sacramental purposes.

It was not the state's first attempt at prohibition, and it would not be the last. Concerns about the effect of alcohol on the Indian community gradually gave way to debates about what kind of moral character the city should keep and how it should deal with public brawls, private domestic unrest and the encroaching poverty of heavy-drinking immigrants.

Secret temperance societies began to organize in Detroit as early as 1830. In 1836, the first meeting of the Detroit Young Mens' Temperance Society resolved to distribute a *Temperance Almanac* to every family in the city. Ten years later, voters in Detroit passed a law prohibiting the grant of liquor licenses. The Common Council tried to appeal it, but the city attorney ruled the law valid and binding.

"The city resolved not to grant licenses. The dealers then resolved to sell," Silas Farmer wrote. Saloonkeepers ignored the law and authorities refused to enforce it, so the city brought back the license system in 1847.

In 1850, Michigan drafted a new constitution, and temperance advocates succeeded in including an article prohibiting the sale of liquor statewide. It was the starter shot in a twenty-five-year tug-of-war between the temperance movement, city government, law enforcement and saloonkeepers.

The city continued to ignore the letter of the law, issuing liquor licenses as though nothing had changed. The only other option was to *not* issue liquor licenses, which brought in cash for the city—and the city knew that the saloons would continue to exist no matter what.

Temperance activists tried everything to get the law to stick. They organized a sort of vigilante enforcement posse, the Carson League, which disbanded in 1853 after Detroit's grocers, hoteliers and barkeeps met at city hall to pass a resolution deeming the Carson League a menace: "We have public officers whose duty it is to administer our laws, therefore we deem any number of persons associated for that purpose to be an illegal society, or league unknown in law, and dangerous to the peace and harmony of the community."

New prohibition laws were passed: the "Ironclad" law of 1855, which declared all payments for alcohol illegal and recoverable by the state; an ordinance in 1858 that required the closure of saloons at 11:00 p.m.; an 1859 law that required each county to hire a chemist as inspector of liquors; and an 1861 law that required bars to close on Sundays.

Nothing changed. Compromises were made and demands scaled back. Winemaking and beer-brewing were legalized. Bar owners continued to do as they pleased. Occasionally, a new temperance law would spook people, and bars would close in droves only to reopen months later. Saloonkeepers and liquor manufacturers were arrested, only to have their cases thrown out by judges who had better things to do. In 1854, when the state's prohibition law was briefly ruled unconstitutional, Detroiters celebrated with a one-hundred-gun salute and, it's safe to assume, a fabulous quantity of booze.

Temperance efforts finally won a little in 1865, when the city finally established its first cohesive (and paid) police force. A notice was posted in the paper after the first Sunday under its authority:

A Quiet Sunday: For the first time in years the great city of Detroit yesterday observed, outwardly at least, the first day of the week with becoming solemnity. All the saloons, bars, and beer-gardens were closed.

Even that effort didn't last. Barkeeps continued to lobby the city to lift the regulations. Temperance societies continued to petition for new laws. This continued, tediously, until 1875, when the article of prohibition in Michigan's constitution was repealed.

All told, the number of breweries doubled, saloons tripled and distilleries quintupled during the first prohibition era.

A DRINK IN DETROIT

We forget about Michigan's first prohibition for a couple of reasons. It wasn't a national experience, first of all; secondly, it was largely ignored. The images of prohibition under the Eighteenth Amendment—rumrunners driving cars across the ice, mob violence and speakeasies—remain salient, and so many Detroiters are personally connected to it. Ask the next person you meet at the bar in Detroit about the Purple Gang—odds are good that her grandfather was mixed up with them or else they gave that grandfather hell. While I was tinkering with my manuscript over a pint of Michigan craft-brewed pale ale, my waitress told me that the Purple Gang drove her Irish Catholic grandfather out of town. I told her that my Russian Jewish grandfather got busted running sugar for his friends in the Purple Gang.

So it's funny that, at the turn of the twentieth century, with a new Detroit on the horizon and a drastic new mood of temperance rolling in like a thunderstorm, business happened in Detroit bars that changed world history.

Malcolm Bingay, an editor of the *Detroit Free Press*, wrote in his memoir, *Detroit Is My Own Hometown*: "Back then, when sports reporters were looking for stories from the leaders of the 'auto game,' they did not ask where these men were; they merely asked, 'Which bar?'"

John and Horace Dodge, founders of the Dodge Brothers engine and chassis company, were hard-drinking brawlers who favored the dingy workingman's saloon over the tony gentlemen's clubs and hotel bars preferred by the city's executives.

After John's death in 1920, Schneider's—the brothers' favorite watering hole—kept a bronze bust of him behind the bar next to a bottle of Noilly Prat vermouth. Sometimes, on especially misty nights, the bartender would pour Dodge's signature martini and waft it under the bust's nose.

FIRST STATE ELECTION

L et's talk about this painting: *The First State Election in Detroit, Michigan, 1837*. The artist: the wayward Thomas Mickell Burnham. The setting: the old state capitol in Detroit, long burned away, the seat of state government anciently removed to Lansing. The star of the show: the Boy Governor Stevens T. Mason, just twenty-six years old, wearing a silken top hat, smoking a cigar and grasping a voter's hand.

It's like Detroit's *Washington Crossing the Delaware*. Only unlike Emanuel Gottlieb Leutze, Burnham actually saw it happen. And, unlike the iconic American painting, everyone in the scene is drunk.

Michigan did not ascend quietly to the Union. In 1831, when he was just nineteen, Mason succeeded his father as secretary of the territory. When Lewis Cass left Michigan that year to join President Andrew Jackson's cabinet as secretary of war, Mason acted as governor, even after Jackson appointed a new governor, George Porter, who spent a lot of time away.

In 1832, Mason began a territorial census. Before its completion in 1834, a devastating epidemic of Asiatic cholera wracked the city, killing nearly one-seventh of Detroit's population, including Porter. Mason, at twenty-two, officially became acting governor. (Mason remains the youngest governor in American history.)

The census confirmed that the territory had a population of more than eighty-seven thousand—way over the minimum requirement for

The First State Election in Detroit, Michigan, 1837 (oil on canvas), by Thomas Mickell Burnham. *Detroit Institute of Arts, USA/Gift of Mrs. Samuel T. Carson/Bridgeman Art Library.*

statehood. The territorial legislature asked Congress for permission to form a state legislature, but Ohio disputed the territorial borders, and Congress rejected the petition.

In 1835, Ohio passed legislation asserting claims to the disputed Toledo strip and forming county governments within its borders. Mason responded with the Pains and Penalties Act, which made it a crime for Ohioans to govern within the strip. Both states called their militias to the border.

No life-threatening casualties were incurred during the conflict that followed, and parties disagreed on whether any shots were ever fired. The "Toledo War" was mostly scuffles between roving posses, citizen arrests and mutual harassment. But President Jackson was concerned that the skirmish could get serious—and he was frustrated with "that young hotspur" Mason. So he removed the governor from office and had him replaced.

Luckily for statehood, nobody liked the new governor, John "Little Jack" Horner, who released war prisoners almost immediately, angering citizens who were already irked by Mason's removal. Just a month after Horner took office, in October 1835, Michigan voters approved the state constitution and elected Mason governor.

Congress wouldn't admit Michigan to the Union until it ceded Toledo to Ohio, and throughout 1836, legislators rejected the president's consolation: the Upper Peninsula. But Michigan was almost bankrupt, and Mason kept pushing for compromise. Finally, in December 1836, a convention in Ann Arbor approved it. Statehood at last!

News that Michigan had become the nation's twenty-sixth state spurred, as such news tended to, celebrations in Detroit's grand old fashion: twenty-six-gun salutes, spontaneous parades, closed businesses, open bars and throngs of sauced-up revelers in the streets. But by the fall of 1837, the glow of pride and cheer had dimmed, and our hero, Stevens T. Mason, was back where all politicians inevitably end up: the slimy maw of politics.

When the curtain opens on Burnham's painting, it's November, and Mason is running for reelection. His opponent is Charles Christopher Trowbridge, a Whig, a prominent pioneer citizen and a former mayor of Detroit. With banks across the nation in tumult and the local economy in a panic, the Whig party is bent on crushing its incumbent contender. Editorials lambast Mason for losing Toledo. Rumors begin to spread that the governor is a hard drinker and a gambler, as well as taking for himself five paychecks a year instead of the prescribed four—detractors dub him "five-quarters Mason." To demonstrate the depth of the state's poverty, Whigs organize a bread line stunt, designating in the morning paper a time and place where they will distribute free food for the poor. (Mostly Irish farmers from Ontario showed up, so the ploy backfired.) Meanwhile, those clever Democrats create a fake third party to try to split the Whig vote. (This strategy also failed.)

It's election day in Detroit, and for some reason there are people with pickaxes everywhere. The streets, as we read in so many contemporary accounts, are just mud. Spooky black clouds are heaving into the rowdy town.

And Mason, shaking hands with that voter? Look a little closer: he's actually passing that voter a buck—for his vote! And the guy behind him is so drunk that he's spilling his jug of whiskey all over the place.

In the lower-right corner rides James Stilson, grand marshal of the Democratic procession, on a horse draped in golden blankets. He's waving a flag that reads: "No Monopoly! Regular Democratic Nomination! Stevens T. Mason for Governor!"

Stilson was one of Detroit's silliest people: a notoriously vain auctioneer who fancied himself a Napoleon although he was tall, blonde and fair. Once he closed an auction of an antique French hand mirror by smashing it with his gavel rather than sell it to a lowballing bidder. In the ultimate fop move, he retired into toy dog breeding. But on election day in Detroit in 1837, he led a grand parade to the center of town, where his company was met by the Whig procession, led by a giant scale model of the schooner USS *Constitution*, which we are at liberty to imagine was a pretty ridiculous thing to drag through those swampy old streets.

One firsthand observer was Joshua Toulmin Smith, a British writer recently arrived in Detroit, who at the sound of cheering in the streets ran to his window with "true English expectations" to see a vast and spectacular crowd. He found only:

> *A long wagon some 20 feet from prow to stern drawn by four clumsily harnessed horses, and all bespattered with mud; in this are seated a dozen drummers and trumpeters, who with infinite skill so contrive to agitate the airy medium that it is quite impossible to distinguish any sequence of tones, at all in accordance with any known melody. Then follows a political emblem the execution of which is well worthy the rude attempts of an infant state, a huge canoe or badly shapen boat mounted on wheels, whereof the sailors perform their characters by diving and rowing the surrounding atmosphere with wooden oars...Of this succeeds another vehicle equally ingenious, for the accommodation of Tory voters whose zeal is either asleep or questionable. These two other common carts drawn by ghosts of horses and their owners in everyday brown coat, followed and surrounded by 30 or 40 ragmuffin looking men and boys all of which look as tho they had escaped from prison, formed the procession which supported Governor Mason in Oct. 1837.*

When the parades met in Capitol Square, there was a great mock battle over the model ship. Except maybe it was a real battle. "Then the fun began," wrote General Friend Palmer, who witnessed the event. Wrote another spectator, Robert Ellis Roberts, the fight resulted in about two hundred casualties—"many bruised heads, black eyes and bloody noses and no fatalities."

So the first state election held in Detroit killed no one, and Mason squeaked to victory over C.C. Trowbridge. The next year, Burnham, a Bostonian who came to Detroit in 1836 to work as a sign painter, left Detroit for greener pastures. It's likely that his painting was meant to ridicule the Mason campaign and local Democratic organizers. It's also possible that he was paid by the Whig party to paint it.

Even though it is satirical and a little ugly, it's also lively and hilarious, and I love it for introducing me to the faces of so many Detroiters I'd never have otherwise known, and a Detroit I barely recognize. Raucous, charged and full of theater, it is a rare window into an otherwise unknowable world—an old, smoky city at its most feverish pitch.

THE RAIN
Good Roads magazine, vol. 2, July 1882

> *We're duly thankful that the rain*
> *Has seen fit to retire,*
> *Though we admit that while 'twas here,*
> *'Twas something to add mire.*

TRAFFIC

In the name of humanity I would inquire whether there is any law or ordinance in this, your city, to prohibit furious driving, and, if there be, whether there is anyone to enforce it?...
Those who want to try the speed of their unfortunate nags, and want to exercise their lungs by unearthly yellings, can go elsewhere.
—letter to the editor, Detroit Free Press, *December 24, 1859*

This is the Motor City, and we are proud of our roads, pockmarked and potholed though they may be. (It's just that we've worn them out with love...right?) We boast the first stretch of concrete-paved road in the country, and our robust system of expressways led to other landmarks, like some of the country's first suburban shopping malls. But our adored streets—a yarn ball of interstates, highways, mile roads and wide, divided boulevards—were hundreds of years in the making.

Silas Farmer painted a colorful picture of street life in the mid-eighteenth century:

> *The streets, in the olden days, afforded many a strange and picturesque sight. Troops of squaws, bending beneath their loads of baskets and skins, moved along the way; rough* coureurs de bois, *with bales of beaver, mink, and fox, were passing to and from the trading stores, and, leaning upon half-open doors, laughing desmoiselles alternately chaffed*

and cheered their favorites; here a group of Indians were drying scalps on
hoops of a fire; others, with scalps hanging at their elbows, dancing the
war dance…staid old judges with powdered cues exchanged salutes with
the officers of the garrison, who were brilliant with scarlet uniforms,
gold lace, and sword-knots; elegant ladies with crimson silk petticoats,
immense beehive bonnets, high-heeled slippers, and black silk stockings,
tripped along the way; and ever and anon the shouts of soldiers in the
guardhouse, made wild with "shrub" and Old Jamaica Rum, were
heard on the morning air, and at times troops of Indian ponies went
scurrying through the town.

Before 1805, the mightiest road in town spanned about twenty feet across; most were less than fifteen feet wide. A promenade, the *chemin du ronde*, ran along the riverfront, but when it was rainy (and it was rainy a lot), the road flooded, and it was back to old-fashioned ways of getting around: on foot, by pony or in a canoe.

Antoine de la Mothe Cadillac came to Detroit with three horses, but two of them died upon arrival, leaving the entire post with one steed, named Colon. If you needed a horse for some farmstead chore—or to be dragged in your sled to the top of a snowy hill—you could rent Colon for the day.

Later, French settlers brought ponies to Detroit, and for a while they were the be-all, end-all of getting around. Farmers branded their ponies and then released them to graze. If you needed one, you could just hike out to the commons and pick one out, according to Palmer, presuming it did not already belong to someone:

The French residents were proverbial for the love they bore their horses;
and the traditional French pony, wiry, strong and fleet of foot, gave them
all they desired in that direction. Every French family owned two or
three ponies, at least, some of them more…Joseph Campau owned a
vast number. Go where you would through the woods adjacent to Detroit,
nearly all of every drove of horses you came across had the letters "J.C."
branded on the flank. So numerous were these ponies that they would
venture into the city in droves during the warm summer nights, attracted
by the salt that the merchants had stored in barrels in front of their
places of business.

These ubiquitous and sturdy creatures were used to pull two-wheeled horse carts, which were a great equalizer; everyone used them, from the working poor to the most fashionable society ladies, who would lay down a buffalo skin and climb in the back. Judge Solomon Sibley was one of the few residents of that old town who had a proper four-wheeled carriage. Just like your one friend with a pickup truck, people were *always* asking to borrow it—people like the venerable governor of the Michigan Territory, Lewis Cass:

> [Cass] *frequently solicited the loan of it, saying to his old French servant, "Pierre! Go up to Judge Sibley, and tell him if he is not using his wagon to-day I should like to borrow it;" and as Pierre started off he would sometimes call after him and say, "Come back, Pierre! Tell Judge Sibley that I am going to get a wagon made, and after that I will neither borrow nor lend."*

So much mixed and unregulated traffic on Detroit's narrow byways—pony carts, horse riders and pedestrians, as well as the old pastimes of horse and carriage racing, which endured from at least the 1750s until the invention of the combustion engine—caused hazardous scenes.

"The streets of that part of Detroit within the stockade are so narrow that foot passengers have difficulty at times to keep clear of horsemen and carriages unless they go slow," noted an 1802 ordinance that forbade fast driving. That ordinance was strictly enforced. Members of the board of trustees that drafted it were among those disciplined for fast horsemanship in some early evidence of Detroit's dragster habits.

The city also had to find a way to keep wandering dogs, cows, fowls and other animals out of the street, leading to the establishment of a city pound-keeper to maintain zoological order. Farmer speculated that pound-keeping might even be Detroit's most "ancient and honorable" profession.

In 1805, the Great Fire leveled the village, and Detroit needed a plan. It was weird luck that the city had just been incorporated under a new administration and established as the capital of the territory; a new governor, Isaac Hull, and two territorial judges, John Griffin and Augustus Woodward, were already on their way. (A third territorial judge, Frederick Bates, was already here.)

Augustus Breevort Woodward is one of Detroit's all-time best eccentrics. A perpetual bachelor and a friend and flatterer of Thomas Jefferson, he favored rumpled suits, showering in the rain, philandering and, even more than most in those days, liquor. Born Elias Woodward, he changed his name to better reflect the imperial and scholarly heritage he felt he had inherited. He studied law, took a shine to speculative science, wrote pamphlets on the substance of the sun and emerging American political theory and disagreed with most people.

Shortly after surveying the fire's damage, Woodward returned to D.C. with Hull and acquired a land grant from the federal government for ten thousand extra acres in Detroit, enough to give every resident a donation lot of up to five thousand feet. Then he went to work on his masterpiece: Detroit's majestic city plan.

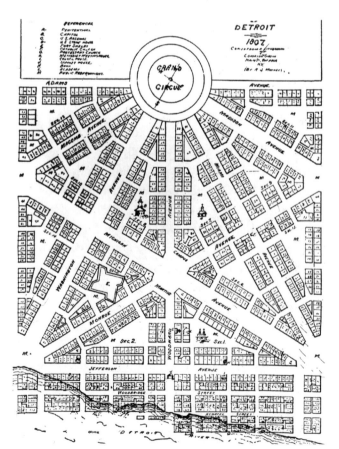

A portion of the Woodward Plan for Detroit after the fire. *Detroit City Plan, 1807. Art, Architecture & Engineering Library Lantern Slide Collection, University of Michigan.*

Riffing on Charles L'Enfant's plan for Washington, D.C. (though some grander minds have imagined Woodward drawing the plat based on his observations of the stars and planets), Woodward sketched out a new city, with one fat road running up into the country at a right angle with the riverfront. This would become Woodward Avenue (because the road, Woodward remarked sarcastically, ran to*ward* the *woods*). He contributed some classical character—the Campus Martius, for instance, named after the public square of ancient Rome. He honored presidents instead of saints, like his friend Jefferson, for whom he named the road that ran along the river. And he envisioned grandeur: abundant full- and half-moon parks, public squares and gridded streets interrupted by broad, angled, tree-lined avenues.

Like Woodward himself, it was not popular. Wrote one visitor:

> *I have seen a plat of this city. I wish, for the sake of the designer, towards whom personally I entertain the kindest feelings, that it had never been conceived by him. It looks pretty on paper, but is fanciful and resembles one of those octagonal spider webs which you have seen in a dewy morning, with a center you know, and lines leading out to the points round the circumference and fastened to spires of grass. The citizens of Detroit would do well, in my opinion, and their posterity would thank them for it, were they to reduce the network of that plan to something more practical and regular.*

It is easy to forget that the Woodward Plan was abandoned in 1811 before it was halfway complete; the modern-day streets of Detroit are baroque as it is, with huge diagonal thoroughfares slicing through the grid streets, cramming at times into awkward triangular intersections and half circles. It is enough to confuse even a regular visitor, but it could have been worse. Wrote Clarence M. Burton:

> *Imagine the present city, with a river frontage of eleven miles, constructed on this plan. A Grand Circus Park every 4,000 feet of that distance and twice as many semi-circular parks and hundreds of triangular parks like Capitol Square and the Public Library. There would be as many squares like the Campus Martius as there were Grand Circus Parks. Even the natives would get bewildered in the labyrinth.*

Visionary, pretentious or both, the Woodward Plan gave Detroit room to grow. And grow it did, but not right away. Streets still weren't paved. Grand Circus Park, the most recognizable and beautiful vestige of the Woodward Plan, was a swamp and a dumping ground as late as the 1840s.

IMPROVEMENTS

Unlike the fire before it—which some historians consider an almost baptismal event, cleansing away the grime and stagnation of the old French era and laying a clean slate for cosmopolitan improvements—the War of 1812 is not generally thought of as a blessing in disguise, and especially not for poor Detroit, so embarrassingly surrendered and only sheepishly returned.

But the war did a few small favors for the city. First of all, it created the first overland routes from Detroit into the territory, across the Ohio Valley and toward the territorial boundaries. The roads were rough—just craggy footpaths or, at best, "corduroy" roads made from felled logs—and they barely improved the wilderness and swamps through which they ran. But they were better than what existed before, namely nothing.

The second grace of the war was that it introduced some new people to the Michigan Territory. Officers, soldiers and volunteers from Kentucky, Virginia, Ohio and Pennsylvania were charmed by the region's rugged scenery—the feral fruit orchards, the miles of glinting shoreline and the prairies and oak groves open for anyone to come settle, build a gristmill, start a family farm or take up a trade. Some stayed. Others went home and told their friends that Michigan was kind of a nice place. Word began to spread.

The signal shot fired from the deck of the *Walk-in-the-Water* on August 27, 1818, was like an announcement to the ages: "Here we go." The first steamboat to sail Lake Erie—and the first to dock in Detroit—slashed travel time from Buffalo, New York, to a lean and reliable forty-eight hours or so. As a basis of comparison, it took Judge James Witherell nearly a month in 1815—after sixteen days grounded on a sandbar, a brief swim when he fell out of a wagon, several miles hiking in the woods

Detroit in 1820 and the steamer *Walk-in-the-Water*, circa 1910. *Library of Congress, Prints & Photographs Division, Detroit Publishing Company Collection, reproduction no. LC-D4-22690.*

to Cleveland, a charter schooner from Cleveland to Detroit, a four-day delay because of headwinds, a storm that stranded the passengers on a river island eating hard peaches and boiled bark, a boat that sprang a leak, an emergency landing in Malden, Ontario, and a final charter service by canoe or rowboat to Detroit.

Even before the Erie Canal, steamboat service on the Great Lakes doubled Detroit's population. When the canal was completed in 1825, about two thousand people lived in the city. By 1836, that many people were arriving in Detroit every day. Not all of them were destined to stay; many were just passing through, by water or by land, to farther points. So Michigan needed roads. It needed a ton of them. And it needed them fast. They were the single biggest obstacle to growth and progress in the territory.

Governor Cass pushed for provisions to create a network of territorial roads, spoking out from Detroit northwest to Pontiac and Saginaw, northeast to Fort Gratiot, west to Ann Arbor, Ypsilanti and Chicago and south to Sandusky, Ohio. Clear some brush, cut the trees lining the route down to stumps, lay down a few logs and there you had it: a road into the wilderness. Still rough, to say the least. But once more, better than the alternative of no roads at all.

A traveler with Reverend George Taylor in 1837 recounted the following story:

> One of these men, a little ahead of the rest of them, discovered, as he thought, a good beaver hat lying in the center of the road, and called his companions to a halt while he ventured to secure it. At the risk of his life, he waded out, more than knee deep to the spot, and seizing the hat, to his surprise he found a live man's head under it, but on lustily raising a cry for help, the stranger in the mire declined all assistance, saying: "Just leave me alone, I have a good horse under me, and have just found bottom; go on, gentlemen, and mind your own business." Such a story, of course, could but have a tendency to heighten in a stranger's estimation, the wonderful attractions of the new State of Michigan.

In the 1840s, with many of the roads built during the first frenzy of internal improvements in the 1820s and '30s falling into neglect, plank roads were proposed. That allowed private owners to charter and operate roads for a small toll. Although many were never completed and some decayed from lack of use, the plank road situation seemed to alleviate the burden of maintenance on the local government and improve ease of access to places like Ypsilanti, Farmington, Howell, Mt. Clemens and Pontiac for settlers who were, very early on, making homes in what we now call the suburbs.

MAINTENANCE

Within the city, it was a different story. When visitors, encouraged by the newly expedient route to the territory, arrived in Detroit, they found a city ill-equipped to deal with an influx of tourists and traffic. Harriet Noble wrote of her arrival in Detroit in 1824:

> For a city it was certainly the most filthy, irregular place I had ever seen; the streets were filled with Indians and low French, and at that time I

could not tell the difference between them. We spent two days in making preparations for going out to Ann Arbor, and during that time I never saw a genteely-dressed person in the streets. There were no carriages; the most wealthy families rode in French carts, sitting on the bottom upon some kind of mat; and the streets were so muddy these were the only vehicles convenient for getting about. I said to myself, "If this be a Western city, give me a home in the woods."

Wrote Captain Frederick Marryatt in 1838:

There is not a paved street in it, or even a foot-path for a pedestrian. In winter, in rainy weather you are up to your knees in mud; in summer, invisible from dust; indeed, until lately, there was not a practicable road for thirty miles round Detroit. The muddy and impassable state of the streets has given rise to a very curious system of making morning or evening calls. A small one-horse cart is backed against the door of a house; the ladies dressed get into it, and seat themselves upon a buffalo-skin at the bottom of it; they are carried to the residence of the party upon whom they wish to call; the cart is backed in again, and they are landed dry and clean. An old inhabitant of Detroit complained to me that people were now getting so proud, that many of them refused to visit in that way any longer.

Marryatt was technically wrong; cobblestone paving projects had begun in Detroit in 1825, but their scope was limited to short stretches of street in front of specific stores or houses. No entire block was paved until 1835.

Fifteen years later, Silas Farmer walked outside and counted "fourteen teams, loaded with wood and other products, stuck fast in the mud on Monroe Avenue, the avenue being only three blocks long." Children who lived less than two blocks from school still had to ride there on horseback; the streets and sidewalks were otherwise impassable.

The pace of paving projects picked up in the 1840s, and by 1849, cobblestone pavement had become widespread. Then, in 1864, Detroit saw its first stretch of woodblock paving.

Wooden pavement had its drawbacks. The lifespan of a woodblock street—best-case scenario—was about ten years. But on a heavily traveled

Lithograph advertisement for Flanigan's Asphaltic and Wood Pavement. *Burton Historical Collection, Detroit Public Library.*

road, it might be more like two or three. Moisture from the rain or other less pleasant elements—horse urine, for example—soaked into the wood, making it liable to rot and reek. Really reek. Also, it was flammable.

But the wood was said to be better than stone at muffling the sound of horse hooves and carriage wheels (and smoother for both carriage and horseback rider). And with a natural abundance of lumber in the region, wood paving was cheap. Throughout the 1870s, due in part to some corrupt municipal contracts for lumber lobbyists, there was "almost a mania for wood pavements." Detroit's serviceable stone-paved streets were torn up and replaced with creosote-treated cedar blocks.

By the 1880s, Detroit streets were once again in deplorable repair. And they were still crowded—they had never ceased to be crowded—with an even broader abundance of traffic: pedestrians, carriages, horse carts, horse-drawn streetcars, omnibuses, taxis and, more recently, bicycles and early prototypes of the automobile. And I'm pretty sure people were still racing horses.

Wrote one witty observer in the *Detroit Post*:

> Detroit has no street signs—that is, no signs with the names of the streets painted upon them. But Detroit has signs of streets. A rough, rotting, unrepaired pavement full of holes, such as jars and rattles the life out of a fine carriage to go over it faster than a walk, is a certain

The first woodblock paving projects began in 1845. By the 1870s, there was "almost a mania" for wood pavement. No. 33 Center Street, Detroit, Michigan. *Library of Congress, Prints & Photographs Division, Detroit Publishing Company Collection, reproduction no. LC-D4-42944.*

sign of a Detroit street. A lake of thin, slippery mud, caused by excessive sprinkling, sending up a continual steam of disease-breeding reek, spoiling the bottoms of ladies' dresses and covering the polished shoes of gentlemen with filth, is a sure sign of a Detroit street. A driveway, nearly half of which is obstructed by piles of brick and building material, and half of the rest by loading and unloading wagons, is another sign of a Detroit street. A passage for teams where everybody digs up the pavement at pleasure to fix a gas or water pipe and puts it down again so as to leave either a hillock or a hole, is another sign of a Detroit street. Utter darkness of nights for two to four blocks, with nobody knows how many holes, piles of rubbish, or other obstructions there may be in the way, so that he has to depend solely upon the intelligence of his horse, is a very common sign of Detroit streets. And finally, to meet with a lost stranger every two or three blocks who stops one to inquire his way, is another continual sign of Detroit streets.

Ultimately, it was the bicycle craze of the 1890s (with some help from that "Idol of the People," Mayor Hazen S. Pingree) that turned this bad situation around.

Rough drafts of the modern bicycle were available in the 1870s, but they were suited for only the sturdy and the brave: your options were the bone-shaker, a ride that rearranged your insides with its rigid cast-iron frame, hard-to-steer front wheel and solid-rubber iron-banded wheels, or the high ordinary, that bike with the perilously tall front wheel. You had to mount it with a stepstool. Once you were atop it, the bike went scary-fast, and a rough patch of road was liable to pitch you over the front handlebars.

It was the safety bicycle, introduced about 1885—coupled with the invention of the air-inflated tire in 1888, which provided desperately needed shock absorption—that finally got people out on the streets. The safety looked a lot like the bikes we still ride today, with a rear-wheel chain drive, front-wheel steering, same-size wheels and a diamond frame.

Bicycling permanently changed the way we get around. Cheaper by scores than a horse (no need to feed it, stable it, bridle it or take it to the veterinarian), bicycles mobilized all manner of Americans. They emancipated women from their houses and from their corsets and voluminous skirts, which they traded in for comfortable shirtwaists and bloomers.

Francis Willard, president of the Women's Christian Temperance Union, learned to ride a safety bicycle at the capable age of fifty-three. Then she wrote a book about it, celebrating its "gladdening effect" and sharing the harrows of traffic:

> *Just as a strong and skillful swimmer takes the waves, so the bicycler must learn to take such waves of mental impression as the passing of a gigantic hay-wagon, the sudden obtrusion of black cattle with wide-branching horns, the rattling pace of high-stepping steeds, or even the swift transit of a railway train. At first she will be upset by the apparition of the smallest poodle, and not until she has attained a wide experience will she hold herself steady in presence of the critical eyes of a coach-and-four. But all this is a part of that equilibration of thought and action by which we conquer the universe in conquering ourselves.*

A young woman, comfortably dressed in a knee-length skirt, with her safety bicycle. Howell, Michigan, 1910. *Burton Historical Collection, Detroit Public Library.*

In Detroit, the bicycle changed the streets themselves. By the 1890s, bicycles were causing as much if not more congestion than any other source of traffic on Detroit's roadways. Wrote Florence Marsh in *History of Detroit for Young People* (a loveable gem of early Detroit history):

> *The city streets were crowded with men, women, and children on wheels... Cass Avenue was so crowded with wheels after dark that the street twinkled with the tiny headlights and the air was filled with the clanging of bicycle bells. Foot passengers waited in vain for a chance to cross the road.*

Cycling advocates founded the Detroit Bicycle Club in 1879, but "[t]here were only a few men who rode bicycles at that time, [and] membership did not exceed twenty," wrote Robert Ross in *Landmarks of Detroit*. In 1880, bicycle activists, enthusiasts and advocates across the nation founded the League of American Wheelmen. Chief among their interests: fixing up nasty old streets so cyclists both avid and casual could use and enjoy them.

The league launched the Good Roads movement, which publicly demonstrated for road improvements, published literature (including *Good Roads* magazine), backed political candidates who supported internal improvements and rallied support from the news media.

In 1890, the Detroit Bicycle Club merged with the Star Club to create the Detroit Wheelmen, a chapter of the national league. Its combined membership of 150 made it one of the largest clubs in the country. When Hazen S. Pingree was elected mayor in 1889, improving Detroit's streets was at the top of his agenda. In six years, Detroit had some of the cleanest, most pleasurable asphalt-paved streets in the nation.

Bicycle use declined when the automobile came on the scene in the early twentieth century. The motor vehicle was a natural outgrowth of the bicycle. Early automotive prototypes, such as Henry Ford's quadricycle, were essentially bicycles with engines on them, and some car pioneers, like the Dodge brothers, were in the bicycle business first. And once the automobile came of age, it had smooth, well-kept roads to make use of. For the Motor City to exist, we needed that motorless two-wheeled wonder, the most efficient mode of transportation ever invented, to pave the way.

The Court Crier Isaac Day

Isaac Day held a number of jobs in early Detroit, including master of the House of Corrections (which doubled as the public weigh house, with Isaac Day its weighmaster), chimney sweep and auctioneer. But his final job was as the crier for the Wayne County Court. He carried a big silver-headed cane, and his primary job seems to have been yelling at people to be quiet. Contemporary accounts allude to his love of whiskey.

He died in 1835, which saddened the court so much that several members of the bar wrote pun-bedecked elegies to his memory. This one is my favorite, by Judge Charles Cleland:

"Step light! The light of Day's expired.
Silent is he who silence oft required.
That stentor's voice and that majestic staff
That raised the bearer and suppressed the laugh
Are heard by Day no more—nor yet by night;
Yet when the evening came, Day still was bright.
But Day today no more shall utter speech,
Since Day's in darkness far beyond our reach.
Alas! Our Day has gone! No ray of light
Bespeak the Day—no morning radiance bright
Shall ever restore to this dark court, its Day.
Darkly they are left to feel this crooked way
Since, as we are told, in Day's report,
Day hath no more Day in court.
None cry for Day, who oft have cried
To please the court, when men were tried.
Yet now that Day's eclipsed, we say,
Peace to his names! Poor Isaac Day."

CEMETERIES

Harvest season in Detroit yielded a macabre crop at the turn of the twentieth century. The *Free Press* reported on October 17, 1914:

> *Souvenir fiends are dashing madly up and down and across Jefferson Avenue, carrying skulls, arrow heads, beads, wampum, bayonets, muskets, locks, horse shoes, brass buttons and other mementos of a gory but historic past.*

This happened all the time. Home builders digging cellars struck the moldering wood of old coffins. Excavators for sparkling new downtown buildings uncovered a hoard of skulls. Curiosity-seekers, profiteers and shopkeepers looking for that *certain something* to put in their window displays loitered near construction sites to see what might turn up.

Newspapers debated whether road paving should happen in the hot summer months, when the incidental discovery of an old graveyard might be especially unpleasant. When a Cass Street paving project was proposed in July 1867, neighbors objected on claims that "in that street still remained large numbers of decaying human bodies which had been buried there in years gone by."

As the *Detroit Advertiser and Tribune* reported, this was not an uncommon problem:

Joseph Campau, a Mason and a wealthy fur trader, was buried in Elmwood after Gabriel Richard excommunicated him from Detroit's Catholic Church. His wife and children are buried in neighboring Mount Elliott Catholic Cemetery. *Photo by the author.*

One gentleman, residing near Howard street, discovered the remains of no less than 14 soldiers while excavating a cellar, and a citizen digging for the same purpose found on the opposite side of the street, some 15 or 16…In laying a drain through the street several years ago similar discoveries were made. The soldiers were often buried in regimental and frequently in cherry coffins. When exhumed the coffins have generally been found in an excellent state of preservation, and the features of the corpses life-like and natural with but little indication of decay, but after a few minutes exposure to the air the bodies crumbled away.

Thus, the paper recommended: "The improvements on the street should obviously be made during the cool season of the year and the remains interred in another locality."

This particular obstacle to progress—the unearthed soldier—presented itself a lot in this neighborhood, roughly bound by modern-day Cass,

Fort, Griswold and Lafayette Streets. That's because there used to be a fort there, hence the name Fort Street. And guess what? Sometimes the fort was used as a graveyard, too. But the military cemetery was not the only burial ground of old Detroit that had been left to erode into oblivion.

Detroit is an old city. And when you study an old city, you watch it unfold from a privileged point in time. You are top of the heap, really—beneath you are generation upon generation of people, as well as the ideas they had, the things they built, the families they raised and the fortunes they won or lost. You come to know and love the people you meet in those books and papers. After a while, they become flesh. You encounter someone as young, vibrant and beautiful—in an old photograph, maybe, where her ringlets of red hair are piled on top of her head and buckled by a silver comb, or in a written account of his sonorous, never-raised voice.

Personally? As soon as those people become real to me, I experience a little grief. The peril of making friends in the halls of history is that all of your friends have died. And some of the things they created that were supposed to be eternal—like their cemeteries—have passed from this earth as well.

A BRIEF HISTORY

Over a few hundred years, a shifting city needs to rearrange itself. To make room for the living, we may have to uproot the dead. Once in a while, we lose track of someone. Sometimes we just build right over the graves. For hundreds of years, Detroiters have written about their cemeteries as if they have been decrepit for hundreds of years.

In 1798, City Registrar Peter Audrain wrote to Arthur St. Clair, governor of the Northwest Territory, to inform him of the sorry state of the graveyard at Ste. Anne Catholic Church:

> *I think it my duty to inform your Excellency that the commandant of this post has granted an acre of ground on the commons joining the town, to be used as a burying ground by the Roman Catholics. This grant answers a very good purpose, as the old burying ground joining their church and within the pickets is so full that it is a real public nuisance.*

General Henry Morrow lamented the condition of the city cemetery on Russell Street before a meeting of the Common Council in 1861:

> *It is little short of disgraceful to Detroit that its cemetery should have been allowed to fall into the ruinous and dilapidated state in which we find it at present. It was once the place of interment for the whole city and in it are deposited the remains of many worthy and respectable people. When the city sold lots in the cemetery, it was with the implied pledge that the grounds should be and remain sacred for cemetery purposes. This pledge has been entirely overlooked or disregarded.*

Silas Farmer—in an uncommonly personal moment—couldn't believe how few historical cemeteries were left:

> *It is a sad commentary on the spirit of the age that there is scarce a grave or gravestone left, or even a record of the present place of burial of those who died at Detroit a century ago. All, all, have disappeared!*

To be fair, Detroit has been burying people for a long time. The story of Detroit's graveyards begins with Ste. Anne, the church that Antoine de la Mothe Cadillac established on July 26, 1701, just days after he arrived to found the French settlement. Catholics of influence, wealth or respect might have been buried on church property—in the graveyard or, for especially worthy members of the fold, in the walls or under the floor of the church.

Protestants had their own burial ground, sometimes called the English burial ground, on the eastern edge of the settlement, which dated to about 1760. Or you might have been buried on or around family property.

Parish control of the main burial ground caused some friction, mostly because no one had any recourse when the church graveyard began to creep across roadways, spill past picket fences or otherwise encroach on public grounds. Nor could anyone do much of anything if the lot became run-down or ill-kept.

So, in 1826, Detroit laid plans for a municipally owned and operated cemetery between Gratiot Avenue and Clinton Street. The first lots were sold at auction in 1828. Clinton Street Cemetery, as it came to be known, had a fence running down the middle to separate Catholic and Protestant burials, along which many families of mixed religious breeding bought plots. The cemetery was a pleasant place for the whole family to enjoy a Sunday outing—it was the closest thing Detroit had to what we now think of as a park. But as the city's population steadily grew—and after a cholera epidemic killed scores in 1832—Clinton Street Cemetery became hazardously cramped. The city opened its second municipal cemetery on Russell Street in 1834.

Less than thirty years later, conditions at Russell Street were already too close for comfort, and the city was slacking in its sacred commitment to tend the ground. No one seemed to be sure who was even in charge. Appealed City Sexton Peter Cliesen to the Common Council in 1857:

> *I respectfully represent to your honorable body, that certain persons are in habit of coming to the city cemetery and digging up bodies for the purpose of removal. Whether they have proper authority so to do I do not know.*
>
> *The cemetery is under my charge and it seems to me proper that bodies should not be dug up except under my direction.*

Four years later, General Henry Morrow complained:

> *Not only has the ground been neglected and the fences allowed to go to ruin, but a portion of the land has been appropriated for other purposes. The city has the power, without doubt, to prohibit further interments in the city cemetery, and it would be its duty to do this if the public health or convenience required such a step. But it is still used for the almost sacred purposes of burial, and yet all care of it is neglected.*

Burials stopped at Russell Street in 1869. Things were a mess, and what's more, the land was starting to look too good to waste on the dead. People were already selling hay and wood at a market nearby, and Gratiot Avenue was the perfect conduit between the city and the country. (Eastern Market, one of the oldest continuously operating farmers' markets in the United States, still stands on the site of Russell Street cemetery.)

When General Friend Palmer visited what remained of the run-down Russell Street cemetery, he imagined what some of its residents would think were they still alive to see it:

Many of our old residents will remember Captain Burtis. His grave is so near Russell Street that the passerby could read his name on the tombstone; doubtless many have done so, when it stood erect, and perhaps have wondered who this person was that once owned the high sounding title of Captain. Quite recently, some miserable vandal broke the stone

A stone angel keeps watch over Woodmere Cemetery, established in 1867. *Photo by the author.*

in twain. The captain had the gift of forcible language to a remarkable degree, and I can imagine him standing beside his own grave, in the flesh, giving vent to his feelings against the perpetrators of the useless act in some of his choicest English.

In 1879, a circuit court ordered the cemetery vacated. From 1880 to 1882, more than 4,500 remains were disinterred and relocated to Elmwood (in a neighborhood east of the city center, the oldest nondenominational cemetery in Michigan), Woodmere (in Springwells, southwest of downtown) and a cemetery on hospital grounds in Grosse Pointe.

WHERE IS LIEUTENANT JOHN BROOKS JR.?

On a dreary fall morning in October 1817, a funeral procession snaked through the streets of Detroit. Attended by soldiers of the Fifth U.S. Infantry and local military and political celebrities—including Major General Alexander Macomb, hero of the Battle of Plattsburgh, and General Lewis Cass, governor of the Michigan Territory—six lieutenants wearing white linen scarves bore the casket on a bier. The somber march ended at Fort Shelby, the star-shaped sentinel at Detroit's muddy heart.

There went trusted leaders, dedicated soldiers, decorated officers and prominent Detroit citizens to lay Marine Lieutenant John Brooks Jr. to rest.

John Brooks Jr. was, everyone agreed, the most beautiful man in Oliver Hazard Perry's fleet. A Harvard graduate and son of Revolutionary War general and governor of Massachusetts John Brooks, the dashing young officer probably wasn't expecting an assignment in the backcountry. But in 1812, Lieutenant Brooks was arrested and found guilty by court-martial for cheating at cards—behavior hardly befitting an elite marine. So it was off to Lake Erie, where the United States was reluctantly preparing a naval defense for its vulnerable inland lakes.

The decisive U.S. victory at the Battle of Lake Erie returned Detroit to American hands. There has never been a more blustery, glorious and gory Great Lakes scene. This was the battle in which Perry wrote to General William Henry Harrison: "We have met the enemy and they are

The Battle of Lake Erie, Commodore O.H. Perry's victory. Lithographed and published by J. Perry Newell, Newport, Rhode Island; printed by J.H. Bufford & Sons, Boston, 1878. *Library of Congress Prints & Photographs Division.*

ours." One reason Perry's victory was so amazing was because he left his destroyed flagship, the *Lawrence*, rowed a small boat under heavy fire to his undamaged *Niagara* and continued to fight the exhausted British fleet. (He brought a blue flag that had flown on the *Lawrence* that read, "Don't Give Up the Ship.")

Fatefully, Lieutenant Brooks was assigned to the *Lawrence*, which the British annihilated. Almost every one of the ship's 136 men was injured or killed, and all of its guns were destroyed.

Brooks was talking to another officer when he was struck by a cannonball and slammed across the boat. The impact shattered his hip and "mangled him in a most frightful manner," but he stayed alive for an hour, bleeding to death and imploring someone to bring him a pistol. No one did.

Most of the thirty sailors killed aboard the *Lawrence* were buried at sea, but three officers from the American fleet—including Brooks—and three British officers were buried the next day on South Bass Island, near Put-in-Bay, Ohio.

Four years later, the Fifth Infantry Regiment of the United States— headquartered at Detroit since 1815—filed a petition to bring Brooks's body to Detroit for a proper military burial:

Resolved unanimously, *that as a tribute of respect, it is due to the memory of Lt. J. Brooks, late of Massachusetts, and of the Marine Corps of the United States, who gallantly fell, on the tenth of September, 1812, while contributing to achieve the splendid victory then gained over the British naval forces on Lake Erie, to remove his remains from Put-In Bay, where they now lie, to this place, for suitable interment.*

Also resolved unanimously, *the officers of the 5th regiment having been generally personal acquaintances of the deceased—knowing his private virtues, and being from the same section of the United States to which he belonged—That it is peculiarly incumbent upon them, as a corps, to perform this duty; and that they will therefore without delay, Maj. Gen. Macomb approving the measure, cause the remains of Lt. Brooks to be removed from Put-In Bay to Detroit, there to be buried, in the Military Burial Ground, with ceremonies and honors due to his rank and worth.*

The regiment also resolved to build a monument to Brooks to honor his memory. General Alexander Macomb approved the measure, and two officers were promptly dispatched from Detroit to Put-in-Bay to retrieve the body. They returned the next day for the funeral.

Reverend Sylvester Larned—brother of Major Charles Larned, a War of 1812 hero who hatched a failed conspiracy against General William Hull to prevent his surrender of Fort Detroit—performed the ceremony, and Captain Henry Whiting of the Fifth Regiment read an elegy:

Too long on lonely isle neglected,
Marked by no stone, thy dust has slept;
By humble turf alone protected,
O'er which rude time each year had swept…

But now, with kindred heroes lying,
Thou shalt repose on martial ground—
Thy country's banner o'er thee flying,
Her castle and her camps around…

Then rest, lamented youth; in honor,
Erie shall still preserve thy name;
For those who fell neath Perry's banner,
Must still survive in Perry's fame.

And so Detroit put the late lieutenant from Massachusetts solemnly to rest.

In less than a decade, Fort Shelby was gone. In 1826, the fort was disused, its pickets decayed and its flagpole long since blown over in a storm. Congress gave it to the City of Detroit to do with it as it wished. Detroit decided to raze it.

What happened to the soldiers and officers buried at Fort Shelby is hard to say. The monument to Brooks's memory was never built, so it's possible that no one knew where Brooks's tomb precisely was. The street commissioner ordered any bones exposed during the demolition disinterred and taken to a burial ground up the block. But that cemetery wasn't long for this world, either. A few years later, all of *those* burials were dug up and removed to Clinton Street.

Obviously, none of this happened too carefully, since forty years later, developers were digging up old graves on and around the old military grounds.

So where is Brooks's body now? Was his one of the lucky skeletons that saw the light of day when Fort Shelby was demolished? He could be anonymously at peace at Woodmere or still in the earth beneath what is now the federal courthouse. He could be washed away—the city used land from the embankment of the fort to grade the level of the river front. Or he could—and this is the official line—still be on that lonely isle neglected.

His name is on the plaque in the rotunda of Perry's Victory and International Peace Memorial at Put-in-Bay, a three-hundred-foot spire commemorating Commodore Perry's glory at the Battle of Lake Erie. When it was constructed in 1912, the six officers buried the morning after the battle were disinterred and replaced beneath the memorial.

Is it possible that the officers from the Fifth Regiment didn't actually find Brooks's remains on South Bass Island and that they just took whatever bones they came across and high-tailed it home?

Did the parks department not know, in 1912, that Detroiters had claimed Brooks as their own, when they set out to find those six officers?

Is it bitterly ironic that the Fifth Regiment's efforts to give its brother Marine a proper burial failed so swiftly and so eternally?

Does all of this just make you think it's all just dust to dust, anyway, and that no towering cenotaph or weeping angel in some rambling old cemetery can change that?

I don't know about you, but I'm leaning toward yes on all of the above.

To the Rag Bag

All beside was new and strange / And change had oft succeeded change.
—Judge James Campbell, "Cassina"

Detroit's relationship with its own past has been reverent and romantic from the beginning. But at least since Father Gabriel Richard first surveyed a territory of illiterate, French-speaking farmers, itinerant traders and marginalized Indians and realized a crucial need for public education—and owing to a location and an economy eternally relevant to the rest of the nation—Detroit has been a place of progress, and our relationship to progress has been proud.

Today, the rest of the world looks on Detroit—once a city of grand hotels, majestic movie palaces and ornate downtown office towers paying dizzying daily homage to the boom of modern industry—with a mixed gut-punch of awe and despair, hope and terror, affection and cynicism. Our leaking, gap-toothed buildings, dropping bricks in the street, some of them scrapped to their shells, seem to admonish the notion that with a little honest work, an American city can catapult its citizens to greater wealth and comfort, stand as an example to the rest of the country and build things the world wants.

But our time is not the first time to furrow a brow toward Detroit's decay. Nor are we the first to fret over the destruction of something old and rickety and in need of tremendous care in favor of something new, promising, less expensive and easier to accomplish.

CASS HOUSE

In 1882, the long-neglected home of Lewis Cass, former governor of the territory and Michigan's most prominent nineteenth-century politician, was demolished. Cass was not the first nor the last to occupy the home. The place seemed ancient—Cass guessed from the bullet holes that pocked its frame that it was built before Pontiac's 1763 rebellion. It was even rumored that Cadillac himself commissioned the house in 1703 as a lodge for the chief of the Hurons. (Better history indicates that a gunsmith, Jean-Baptiste Baudry, built the house about 1750 on lands he acquired from the Huron tribe.)

The stooped and rustic log house, made of oak and sided with hand-split clapboard, was originally built on the riverfront. In 1836, the riverfront was graded down, and the house was cut in half and moved to Larned between First and Second Street.

In 1882, on the eve of its demolition, visitor Thomas McKenney shared his impressions of the governor's comfortable but oddly woodsy

The Lewis Cass House, date unknown. *Burton Historical Collection, Detroit Public Library.*

place—more home on the range than gubernatorial *palais royale*. The salon was strewn with Cass's papers, the walls were hung with Indian relics—"pipes, snowshoes, medals, bows, arrows"—and the whole house was warmed from a stove in the dining room:

> *There is much of the simplicity of republicanism about all this. Extrinsic appearances are to a reasonable extent disregarded, and the higher value is attached to the interior. And this is not an unfit emblem of the governor himself.*

In other words, don't judge a book by its cover. But what was *that* supposed to mean about the governor's "extrinsic appearance"? Witness this masterful backpedaling:

> *You are not to imagine, however, that this is intended to apply to his person, that is portly and altogether governorlike, and in regard to which he is neat in his dress and though plain, polished in his manners.*

General Friend Palmer also reminisced about the Cass House when it was scheduled to come down:

> *One thing I remember in particular was the large knocker on the front door. It was a lion's head in bronze, had a large ring through its nose for a clapper. It was there when the governor took the house. There was a deep mark across the lion's face, as if made by some sharp instrument wielded by a powerful hand. The general used to say, he was told that it was made by Chief Pontiac, who, after a stormy interview with the then occupant of the house, who was commandant at that time in Detroit, left in high dudgeon and when the door had closed upon him, he drew his tomahawk from his wampum belt and dealt the lion's head a fierce back-hand blow with it that left a mark.*

Cass was rumored to have taken the lion's head with him when, after an appointment to President Andrew Jackson's cabinet, he moved out of the house in 1831. After he left, the house passed to new owners and then to speculators, and eventually the land it sat on was more valuable than the house itself.

Many wanted to save it. In 1882, the *Detroit Evening News* published its opinion that "the eminent and historic associations of the structure should have reserved it for a better fate than has befallen it." Others resigned the Cass House to the scrapheap of progress and industry.

Palmer lamented that no one really seemed to care *what* happened to the house—at least not enough to do anything:

> *At the time of the demolition of the Cass* [House], *it was suggested by some one that the City of Detroit buy it and remove it to East Grand Circus Park, but no one in authority took any interest in the matter, the idea died out and the old historic relic went to the rag bag, so to speak.*

Judge James Campbell wrote an elegy, "Cassina," on the event of its demise. It is far too sweeping a work to include in full, but here is the introduction and the coda:

> *Half hid beside the noisy street,*
> *Gray with old storms and summer's heat,*
> *The ancient house seemed all alone,*
> *Hemmed in by walls of brick and stone,*
> *But straight its roof, its frame was sound*
> *From gable peak to level ground,*
> *Of sturdy beams so square and stout*
> *That time could never wear them out;*
> *For many a frigate safely rides*
> *With lighter keel and frailer sides.*
>
> *Strangers would pause to ponder o'er*
> *The low browed eaves and deep set door,*
> *And wondering ask what freakish fate*
> *Had saved the homely pile so late,*
> *When all beside was new and strange*
> *And change had oft succeeded change....*
>
> *The spreading town has shouldered*
> *The useless fort away,*

The grasping hands of Commerce
   Are closing on the bay,
The garden and the orchard,
   No ripened fruit retain,
And idlers cross the wheat-fields
   And trample down the grain.
Alas for the brave old mansion!
   Alas for its ancient fate!
Old things make room for the present
   As ashes follow the flame.
But all of the massy timbers,
   Are sound and stiff and strong,
And in their seasoned fibre lies
A store of precious memories,
That, wakened by the sounding bow,
May murmur music sweet and low,
   Or quiver into song.

CAMPAU HOUSE

No one personified Old World, old-fashioned, frontier French Detroit like Joseph Campau. Born in 1769, Campau was a third-generation Detroiter. His grandfather served under Antoine de la Mothe Cadillac. His father sheltered British soldiers during the Battle of Bloody Run.

Courtly Campau—with his stiff black suit, white cravat and heavily accented, French-peppered English—was a common sight on the streets of Detroit for decades, mumbling to himself and greeting neighbors with a hearty "Bonjour!"

Local Indians knew him as *Chemokamun* ("Big Shot"). From his post on the first floor of his house, Campau traded all manner of goods from Montreal and Boston—rifles, shot, bullet molds, gunpowder, glass beads, tin buckles, silver earrings, bracelets, blankets, plates, frying pans, fabric, needles and thread and, of course, sugar, alcohol and tobacco—for furs, which were shipped to London and France and sold for a fortune.

By 1880, Joseph Campau's pioneer homestead on Jefferson Avenue was completely overshadowed by more modern commerce. Jefferson Avenue, circa 1880. *Burton Historical Collection, Detroit Public Library.*

When his nephew—future Detroit mayor John R. Williams—was fourteen years old, Campau left him in charge of the shop while he traveled for business. He also left this advice:

> *Keep your goods well assorted and do not allow the other merchants to get the start of you in this in my absence. Try to be patient with the savages, so as not to drive them from the shop. Always be discreet in business, anything else is fatal...You may give credit to those who you know are capable of paying. Take all kinds of grain at the current price, but chiefly wheat. Try to make those pay who owe me and neglect nothing.*

A shrewd investor, Campau owned a distillery, interest in a fledgling railroad company, thousands of acres of land and a founding share of the

Detroit Free Press. His house was a fixture of the old city—a log cabin held together with hickory pegs instead of nails, painted yellow and white. The front doors, in the Dutch style, were divided horizontally to let breezes in, keep animals out and encourage leisurely afternoon leaning. Campau built this house in 1813, but preservationists invoked the mythical age of the place with claims that it was built on one of Cadillac's original land grants and that its foundations were laid before the Great Fire of 1805.

All of this may have been true. But Campau's home was a distinctive signal that times had changed, were changing and would always change. As Detroit grew, fur trading and general stores gave way to goliath manufacturing operations and specialty goods, and the newfangled industrial city of the 1860s—with its tall stone buildings and wood-paved streets—engulfed the Campau homestead. Wedged on a busy downtown business block, it stood as an adorable anachronism, a specter of an older era and a valentine to how far Detroit had come.

Remembering the house with more than a little nostalgia in 1894, George C. Bates wrote:

> *During the last sixty-three years of that long and interesting life he resided in the old house on Jefferson avenue between Griswold and Shelby streets, which is as notorious today as the falls of Niagara, and which all the young and bustling driving business men of Detroit might visit with pleasure and profit. There they may learn prudence and care by examining an umbrella manufactured in Philadelphia in 1802; an anvil hammered on in his blacksmith shop in 1805; furniture manufactured in his own cabinet shop in 1797; unpaid accounts beautifully prepared and endorsed against men who died in the last century, every paper and record filed in the neatest possible manner...an old working desk deeply scalloped out by Campau's left knee, which year in and year out rubbed against it, a large curvature in the windowsill produced by the same attrition, photographs taken years since of his children—everything there just as he placed it long ere nine tenths of the people of Detroit of today were born.*

The Campau House stayed in the family until Joseph's son, Denis Campau, died in 1878, leaving no heirs. Francis Palms, who bought the house, wanted to tear it down to build a hotel.

"It is not too late for the city to secure the old homestead, as Mr. Palms stands ready to donate it should the authorities consent to accept it," wrote the *Free Press*. "The Campau homestead as a relic of the earliest days of Detroit is more interesting than any other building within its limits, and the building really ought to be preserved." It was not preserved. Demolition began in 1879.

HAMTRAMCK HOUSE

Jean-Francois Hamtramck, the first American commander of Fort Detroit, was born in Quebec in 1756. Before he was twenty, he had joined American forces fighting for independence from the British. He was in active duty for the rest of his life. Hamtramck played a major role in securing the Northwest Territory during the Indian Wars of the early

The romantic and ramshackle Colonel Jean-Francois Hamtramck House became a popular place for picnics, paintings and picture-taking before its demolition in 1891. Pictured here, believe it or not: Jim Scott and his wife, 1881–91. *Burton Historical Collection, Detroit Public Library.*

1790s. George Washington personally commended him for his bravery more than once. In 1796, the Jay Treaty passed control of Detroit from British to American forces, but General "Mad" Anthony Wayne was too ill to make the journey to raise the flag, and he left Colonel Hamtramck in charge. Hamtramck, a slight man who was said to prefer riding the tallest horse he could possibly find, looked very silly at the head of his men ("Crooked like a frog on horseback," said Major Ambrose Whitlock). But he was beloved by his men, heralded as a patriot and adored by Detroiters.

Hamtramck bought some riverfront property in 1802 on a farm two miles east of the city, not far from Belle Isle, and built a modest one-story wooden house with a chimney on either side. He died the following year, leaving a humble estate for his widow. She remarried and moved to Indiana.

The house stood for the better part of a century after Hamtramck's death, and several owners occupied the quaint historic home. But eventually, the Hamtramck House met a predictable fate: the history of the house wasn't enough to make it livable, the charm of its age and its lack of modern amenities wasn't cute anymore and it fell into disrepair.

The ruins of the Hamtramck House had loads of romantic appeal. It was a popular subject for painters and picnickers. It was also enjoyed by scrappers and vandals, according to reports of its decline. An 1892 article in the *Free Press* documented the decline of the Hamtramck House:

> *Racked and broken with age and ruined by vandals and hoodlums…The window panes are all broken, the shutters have been wrenched off…and portions of the weather board have been taken away…*
>
> *At present it is in a dilapidated condition, which is caused more by the vandalistic propensities of young hoodlums than the hand of time.*

The Hamtramck House was finally demolished in 1898.

You couldn't open a newspaper in the 1890s without confronting news of some worthy home—a little clapboard shack built in the French era or a grand stone mansion built by a magnate—coming down to make way for new development. We'd consider many of them pricelessly historic now. But some weren't even that old by Detroit standards—built in the 1830s or 1840s and torn down forty or fifty years later—like the Duffield House, where the Reverend George Duffield and his wife, Isabelle Bethune, celebrated their fiftieth wedding anniversary in 1867. Reverend Duffield had performed "innumerable" weddings in that house, but "commercial interests are iconoclastic in their progress, and partake little of sentiment," wrote the *Detroit Post & Tribune* in 1883, the year it was torn down. The house was thirty-eight years old.

Progress, that complicated animal, never stops for fond feelings. But in newspaper notices and the sad essays of contemporary historians, you catch a glimpse of how fast Detroit's neighborhoods were changing, as well as how the pace of that change stunned—and stung—the aging citizens of the city on the straits.

Captains of Industry

What did Detroit make before it made cars? *Lots* of things: stoves, lumber, salt, ships, spirits, tobacco, pharmaceuticals and more, each product pushing Detroit's pin on the map a little deeper, enticing a few more people to pack up their worldly belongings and head to the city to try something new.

Some were swindled and some just got by. But a few played their cards right—or were dealt winning hands to begin with—and walked away with a jackpot. A few of them even left Detroit in better shape than they found it. Others just left a good story to tell. It takes all kinds.

Silver Heels

You can meet Colonel David McKinstry in the painting *First State Election in Michigan*. He's the one next to a huddle of newspaper reporters, wearing a tall beaver hat, holding a cane, his shirt collar unbuttoned. At his feet is a billet for his circus. His hair is gray, his aspect refined and his face firm, forward-looking and slightly smirking.

Colonel McKinstry (or was he a major—no one agrees) was Detroit's amusement king. And like Ozymandias, his empire, though perhaps the most astounding of its time, has disappeared.

Look on his works, ye mighty, and despair: the colonel built the entertainment epicenter of early Detroit. Michigan Garden was opened in 1834, its four acres arrayed with fruit trees and flowers from all over the world. Its wandering walkways were brilliantly lit at night and filled with floats of music from the house band and the sound of dishes clattering in the Garden's restaurant.

Attached to the Garden was a small menagerie, which included such suspect attractions as this event, advertised in an 1835 paper:

> *Rare sport at the Michigan Garden! Two bears and one wild goose will be set up to be shot at, or chased by dogs, on Tuesday, 20th October, at two o'clock P.M.*
>
> *N.B.—Safe and pleasant seats will be in readiness for Ladies and Gentlemen.*

The colonel also operated a theater, a circus and a museum, among the first in Detroit, "consisting of some of the finest specimens of ornithology, minerals, coins, natural and artificial curiosities, and a Grand Cosmorama occupying one building of the Garden, another containing thirty-seven wax figures of some of the most interesting characters."

The museum was not the only first of its kind McKinstry brought to Detroit. He was also responsible for the city's first bathtubs—an elegant and commodious addition to hygienic life in the old city. Before the public bathhouse at the Garden, you would have bathed once a week in the wooden washtub you used at home for your laundry, your dishes and scrubbing your floor.

Besides his business endeavors in botany, bathing technology, zoology, curiosities and traveling vaudeville shows, McKinstry was involved in a number of city- and state-building enterprises, serving variously as captain of Fire Engine Company No. 1, inspector of the port, city alderman, superintendent of the poor and on contract for the construction of the territorial capitol and the Saginaw Road.

Are you impressed yet? If not, consider the *Olive Branch*, his horse-boat to Canada, propelled through the waters of the Detroit River by two French ponies walking in place on tread wheels that turned beneath their hooves to power the paddle wheel on the side of the boat. (One writer described it as looking like "sort of a cheese box on a raft.") The *Olive Branch* was launched from McKinstry's wharf in 1825, ferrying travelers and their wagons, horses and cattle from shore to shore for the next five years.

McKinstry's many and varied business pursuits—which in his later life included stagecoach lines, bigger and better river steamers and investment in the emerging railroad economy—must have been lucrative. The business advantage, personal presence and minor fortune he amassed in Detroit earned him the nickname "Silver Heels."

McKinstry bootstrapped that gleaming reputation. When he came to Detroit from Hudson, New York, in 1815, he didn't have any money or a bankable trade. But he was a hard worker and an ambitious guy, and it didn't take long for him to make a name for himself in the small, scrappy harbor town. Detroit, after all, tended to reward the resourceful, the flinty and the fearlessly industrious. In a letter to a friend dated September 11, 1840, former territorial governor William Woodbridge recommended McKinstry as "a man of very considerable shrewdness and business talents—of much energy of character—quite disposed to speculation and not over scrupulous of means."

The colonel's museum, his wood-frame circus, his theater and most of his other entertainment properties burned down in a disastrous New Year's Day fire in 1842. Not long afterward, he invested in some land in Ypsilanti, thirty miles west of the city, and eventually moved into the hotel he built there. Woodbridge speculated that the colonel may have fallen out with some of his business partners and perhaps—just perhaps—might have been "of doubtful capacity" to meet his financial obligations.

He died in 1856. He was seventy-eight years old.

THE GHOST

Daniel Scotten was thirty-four years old and working as a bookbinder in Palmyra, New York, when he decided it was time for a change. He took all the cash he had—about $1,500—and got on a boat. Not long after he landed in Detroit, his money was tied up in the industry he'd deemed most likely to grow: tobacco.

Tobacco boomed in Detroit during the late 1800s. An 1884 advertisement for American Eagle Tobacco shows a portrait of actress and celebrity spokeswoman Lily Langtry dressed as a geisha. *Library of Congress Prints & Photographs Division, LC-USZC2-5739.*

Scotten's wager was either lucky or shrewd, as in the next several decades, Detroit became a tobacco boomtown, and by 1891, it was the city's leading industry. Splendid quantities of the stuff grew in southern Ontario, and it was cheap to import. As Detroit had yet to become a union town, costs for labor were low, too.

The same year he arrived, Scotten established a partnership with Thomas C. Miller and cofounded Thomas C. Miller & Company Tobacco. Three years later, Scotten sold his share to Miller, bought out another tobacco firm, wrangled some partners and founded Scotten, Granger & Lovett. Years passed, partnerships shuffled, business boomed and Scotten eventually built a huge factory on Fort Street to house the Scotten & Company manufacturing operations— makers of Hiawatha Tobacco.

Hiawatha was one of several leading brands of Detroit cigars, cigarettes and chew: others included Globe, American Eagle, Banner and Mayflower, helmed by future Michigan governor John Judson Bagley.

Detroit tobacco made Scotten an outrageously wealthy man, and as some outrageously wealthy men sometimes do, Scotten reinvested his wealth into real estate, making him even more outrageously wealthy. His most prominent property was the glamorous and cosmopolitan Hotel

Cadillac on tony Washington Avenue. Every week, Scotten drove his carriage, hauled by two white horses, to collect rent at the hotel, usually stopping at the bar to enjoy a drink from a "special" bottle kept behind the counter just for him. He also owned seven thousand acres of farmland and 1,800 head of cattle in Petite Cote, Ontario.

At his own home in Detroit, he raised hens and turkeys, which he gave away to friends (including Clarence M. Burton—maybe to gain the favor of posterity?) and strangers as holiday gifts. Another distinctive sight in the Scotten backyard was a towering pile of lumber, a help-yourself stash for anyone who was suffering the tough winter months without fuel for warmth.

Does it sound like Scotten was a little eccentric? It's not your imagination. Detroiters admired and respected "Uncle" Daniel Scotten—the classic mold of a self-made man and a genuinely charitable person who not only doled out massive cash gifts to worthy institutions but also personally distributed clothing and food to those in need.

They also thought he was kind of a nut. Alarmingly well read, Scotten kept thousands of books in his home library, loved Shakespeare, studied anatomy, literally read the dictionary for fun and visited his local florist just to argue about the Latin names of the weeds in his garden.

"For a man who has a number of millions of dollars, Daniel Scotten lives the life of a hermit and works like a horse," wrote the *Detroit News-Tribune* in an 1896 profile. Scotten was nearly seventy-seven years old. "He speaks business in words of one syllable, such as: *I will, I will not, yes, no, all right, good day.*"

Oren Scotten, Daniel Scotten's nephew, was born in New York in 1850 and came to Detroit when he was sixteen. Naturally, he asked his magnate uncle for a job. Allegedly, Scotten said, "Take off your coat and work, then." And Oren, not sure what else to do, picked up a broom and started sweeping the floor. Oren's humble start at Hiawatha eventually led to a partnership with his uncle.

In 1898, when Daniel Scotten was a spry eighty years old, Oren became an incorporating member of the Continental Tobacco Company, a holding company whose shares were mostly owned by American Tobacco. The Scotten Company became the "Northwest Branch" of

Continental Tobacco, and Daniel Scotten retired to the tune of $2.5 million (a staggering $64 million today).

In 1899, Daniel Scotten died of "extreme age," according to his obituary in the *New York Times*. But the old millionaire's soul would not rest, legend said, until his factory, which was temporarily closed shortly after his death, was blazing again. Wrote Stephen Bromley McCracken:

At one time two servants employed at the former dwelling were passing through the roadway to Porter street, when the figure of a man, white and terrible, came out from behind the barn. To their excited imaginations it appeared to be the ghost of Daniel Scotten, but on his face was a scowl as he turned and gazed at the chimneys of the disused factory. With loud screams the servants made tracks for the street and notified patrolman Purcell, who examined the grounds, but could find no ghost. Since then it is claimed that the wraith appeared several times. It is even rumored that he has been heard to say, Ever more must I walk until the smoke comes out of the chimneys of the old plant. *Superstitious neighbors remember that Mr. Scotten used to make nocturnal trips about the house grounds with a lantern to see that all the doors were properly closed and the watchmen attending to their duties…Anyway, since the works have been reopened, it be said, as Hamlet said to his father's ghost,* Rest, rest, perturbed spirit.

As for Daniel Scotten—in life—he preferred to be remembered by his good works alone. For his obituary in the *Detroit Journal* on March 4, 1899, a close friend is reported to have said:

Detroit doesn't need any fountain, or monument, or memorial building to keep Uncle Daniel in its hearts…Several generations of people will have to pass away before your Uncle Daniel will be forgotten. And Detroit doesn't want, in the future, to have the mannish woman or womanish man raise an eye-glass towards a monument and exclaim: Ah! What is that! Who was he!—Oh, some rich old duffer who died a few generations ago…Daniel Scotten should be paid the tribute of having nothing erected to his memory by the present generation.

THE CLOCKMAKER

Felix Meier sailed to the United States from Germany in 1864. It was a grueling journey: the boat was crowded, food supplies were perilously low and Meier's wife was pregnant. She gave birth to their son, Louis, on board the ship.

Meier was a stonemason by trade, and when he arrived in the United States he worked on railroad bridges. He briefly moved to Chicago in 1871 to rebuild after the fire that leveled the city that year.

Stonecutting was a respectable trade, but the level of craftsmanship was considered to be somewhat rough. Not bad for a day job, but Meier had finer dreams. In the evenings, as a hobby, he made watches and clocks. And one Sunday, while napping on a davenport, Meier dreamed of his masterpiece: the American National Astronomical Clock.

Felix Meier's American National Astronomical Clock, date and original publication unknown. *Burton Historical Collection, Detroit Public Library.*

He started to build it about 1870, and it took him ten years to complete. When it was finished, it was a baroque wonder: eighteen feet tall, four thousand pounds, intricately carved from black walnut, its machinery demandingly precise.

At the top of the clock was a marble canopy. Atop the canopy, a gilded statue of Columbia. Beneath the canopy, the seated figure of George Washington. Adorning the four corners of the clock were the phases of life, each of which marked a quarter hour with a distinct bell: the infant, the youth, the middle-aged man and the old man. In the center of the clock was the figure of a skeleton, which struck the hours with "a deep, sad, tone." And then (according to Silas Farmer):

> *When Death strikes the hour, a music-box concealed within the clock begins to play; the figure of Washington rises slowly from his chair and extends the right hand, presenting the Declaration of Independence; the door on the left is opened by the servant, and all the presidents from Washington to Hayes enter in procession, dressed each in the costume of his time. Passing before Washington, they raise their hands as they approach him, walk across the platform, and disappear through the opposite door, which is promptly closed by the second servant. Washington then resumes his chair, and all is again quiet, save the measured tick of the huge pendulum.*

Meier's great clock was also a marvel of astronomical clock-making; some enthusiasts considered it one of the most accomplished astronomical clocks ever made.

It told local time, as well as time in nineteen major world cities from Paris to Peking, Cairo to Constantinople. It indicated the house of the zodiac, the revolutions of the earth on its axis, the revolutions of the moon around the earth, the phases of the moon and the movement of the planets around the sun. ("There is, therefore," one reporter wrote breathlessly, "a movement in this wonderful piece which cannot regularly be completed more than once in 84 years!"—because Uranus takes eighty-four years to orbit the sun.) Meier's calculations were so precise, he claimed, that they would be accurate for two hundred years.

The clock went on a yearlong U.S. tour. By the time the tour was over, the clock still worked, but Meier was broke. Shipping the enormous clock around the country had eaten into the profits from the tour. It was also rumored that Meier was a gambler. Debt-mired, he was anxious to sell the clock to the highest bidder.

What became of Meier's American National Astronomical Clock—"undoubtedly the most famous clock ever constructed," wrote one biographer—is unclear.

In 1880, Meier sold his share of the clock for $1,000 to Jennie Babcock of New York City. Clarence M. Burton reported that the clock was displayed in the Tiffany's showroom for twenty-five years. But that's impossible. In 1895, Meier received a letter from Eliza Thayer, who told him that Mrs. Babcock had passed away, and although she had found some interested buyers for the clock, the offers were low and the clock was in storage—dusty, defaced and in need of repair.

"I long to see this wonder," Thayer wrote, "where it can be <u>observed</u> and <u>known</u>. Can your services be obtained to restore it to running order, either as it is placed in New York City or in Washington?"

Meier wrote back and asked for the lowest price at which she would sell, as well as the percentage she would offer him as commission were he able to secure a buyer. Negotiations with Ms. Thayer fell through. In 1907, a year before he died, Meier's astonishing astronomical clock was destroyed in a New York City warehouse fire.

But it was not the end of the Meier clock dynasty. Felix's children turned out to be just as ingenious. His son Felix Jr., at nineteen years old, perfected a compact steam engine that he mounted on a buggy and drove around the streets of Detroit during the early days of the automotive era. His son Andrew, at twenty, invented a carpet-cleaning machine. Both Felix Jr. and Andrew died young, but Felix's son Louis would send the Meier name into the new century.

Louis built his own astronomical clock—Louis Meier's Wonderful Clock, a similarly astounding work of craftsmanship: fifteen feet high and seven feet wide, with a twelve-inch globe that revolves on its axis every twenty-four hours. Father Time strikes a chime at the top of the hour. He completed it in 1904; it was exhibited at the Michigan State Fair in 1906, and by all accounts, the clock demonstrated the continued vitality of the Meier clock brand. Louis Meier went on to open a small jewelry, watch and clock shop in 1914. By the 1930s, Meier and Sons was manufacturing commercial gears, and the company produced arsenal components during World War II.

Louis Meier's Wonderful Clock met a much kinder fate than his father's invention: it's on display and remains in full working order at the Detroit Historical Museum.

DAUGHTER OF INDUSTRY

Eber Brock Ward began his career as a cabin boy on a Great Lakes schooner in the employ of his uncle Captain Samuel Ward. He was thirteen years old. When he died, he was one of the richest men in the Midwest.

He came to Detroit in 1821, when it was still a rough-and-tumble port town of about 1,400 people. Great Lakes ships were pretty small then, and most of them were British-owned. None was owned by Detroiters.

He bought his first share in a steamboat—the *General Harrison*—in 1835, when he was twenty-four years old. By the mid-nineteenth century, Captain Eber B. Ward and his uncle, Captain Sam, had a fleet of thirty ships and were the largest shipowners on the Great Lakes.

As industrial enterprise expanded in Detroit and Michigan, Eber Ward was involved with everything. Lumber? He owned seventy thousand acres in northern Michigan and built his own sawmill—the finest in the country. Steel? He started the Eureka Iron and Steel Company in 1853. It was the first American firm to use the fast, inexpensive Bessemer process to make commercial steel. Railroads? As president of the Pere Marquette Railway in 1860, Ward lifted the struggling company out of bankruptcy and dysfunction. His lumber and metal were used for making new railroads. He opened a steel mill in Illinois and another in Milwaukee. He built a lumber mill in Toledo. He built a shipyard in Wyandotte, Michigan. He started a plate glass company. He bought a few newspapers. He bought a salt mine and a silver mine. And in 1875, while he was walking down Griswold Street, he had a stroke and dropped dead.

Captain Ward's death stunned the region. "His immense wealth and business interests were such that hardly a city of any importance in the Northwest but will be more or less affected by his death," wrote the

Western Historical Company in *History of St. Clair County, Michigan.* "His enterprises extended through a number of states reaching from the cold and icy northern shores of Lake Superior to the warm waters of the Gulf of Mexico."

At his death, the total value of his estate—dizzyingly entangled in a vast array of accounts, companies and properties—was tough to guess, but $10 million is probably fair. (That's close to $200 million, adjusted for inflation, based on the 2010 consumer price index.)

He also left behind an expansive family—a wife, an ex-wife and seven children. His youngest, Clara, was just two years old. She inherited a significant chunk of her father's lumber interests and grew up, predictably, in luxury. She moved with her family to New York, attended private school in London and as a teenager made an aristocrat-hunting tour of southern Europe with her mother, Eber Ward's second wife and widow, Catherine Lyon.

In 1890, a Belgian prince and diplomat, Marie Joseph Anatole Pierre Alphonse de Riquet, Prince de Caraman-Chimay, proposed to Clara Ward. She was seventeen years old when they were married in Paris.

The Prince de Chimay got the better end of the deal, at least at first. His title was real, but he didn't have much in the way of royal fortunes. His chateau needed extensive repairs, and Clara spent $100,000 of her inheritance to pay off his debts. Belgians gossiped that King Leopold favored Clara Ward a little too keenly, and court society shunned her.

To escape the harsh talk, Clara and her prince moved to Paris, where they enjoyed the artistic, absinthe-tinted Belle Époque nightlife.

In 1896, in one of those jangly cafés, Clara met Rigó Jancsi, a swarthy Hungarian violinist with piercing eyes and dark, romantically unkempt hair. It was love at first sight, the tabloids reported to a frankly baffled public. Clara and her "gypsy" ran off together, scandalizing everyone and catapulting each other to instant celebrity. (The Prince de Chimay sought a divorce.) Tabloids tracked their every move. Rigó played salons and music halls across the continent, and Clara—inspired, perhaps, by her second husband's art—performed at the Folies-Bergere, the Moulin Rouge and dozens of other cabarets. Her gimmick was the *pose plastique*—in a skintight, flesh-colored body suit, she struck a comely posture and then stood stone-still. Titillating, right?

Sultry Clara Ward postcards circulated Europe. Hungarians commemorated the scandalous romance by inventing a chocolate cream pastry called the *Rigó Jancsi*. Toulouse-Lautrec painted them when they appeared together at the theater.

While she was partying in Europe's capital cities decked in diamonds and furs, gossip rags sniveled that she was bleeding millions, living only to serve her own selfish desires. I wonder if the truth was more complicated than that. She was all but disowned by her wealthy Detroit family, paying alimony to her children with the Prince of Chimay and fighting constantly with Rigó, who allegedly owed her hundreds of thousands of dollars.

Detroiters thought that their city had arrived when Europe's bluebloods started poaching industrial heiresses for wives. With every princess crowned, an American fairy tale came true. But some happy endings faded into ennui, disappointment and drama. Martha Palms, the Countess de Champeaux, died young. Matilda Cass Ledyard, Lewis Cass's granddaughter, married Baron Clemens von Ketteler, a German ambassador to China, who was gruesomely killed (his heart was ripped out and eaten) during the Boxer Rebellion after attacking and murdering, for no discernable reason, a young Chinese civilian.

I know some ladies (or their gold-digging moms and dads) went looking for this supposedly sweet setup, but can you imagine moving thousands of miles away from your family to a country where you don't speak the language to shack up with some older man you barely know whose drafty palace hallways faintly smell of the collapse of European empire?

It's hard to feel bad for Clara Ward, but I don't think her life was easy. From her father, besides her millions, it seemed she had inherited a personal propensity for homefront disaster. Eber Ward's first marriage ended in divorce after his wife accused him of serial adultery. His children from both wives were born with demons. His son Charles was "deranged and eccentric," as well as bankrupt; Henry Ward was committed to a state mental institution; and Frederick Ward committed suicide.

Clara and Rigó divorced in 1904. Clara got married again, this time to Peppino Riccardi, an Italian travel agent. Riccardi accused her of having an affair, and they separated in 1911.

She was forty-three years old when she died at her villa in Padua, possibly of pneumonia. Though reports from Rome of her funeral stated that she was buried a pauper—her only asset a cheap case of jewels seized by creditors—the American consul at Venice wrote to relatives in the United States and assured them that Ms. Ward's funeral was "elaborate and costly." In a will drafted in 1904, Clara left an estate worth more than $1 million to Riccardi and her two children in Belgium.

Wrote the *Detroit News* in her obituary:

> *A score of years ago, Clara Ward was the idol of Detroit young womanhood. Wealthy and beautiful, she left her native Detroit to marry the Prince de Chimay and Caraman, a Belgian nobleman closely allied to the royal family. Her light burned brightly in the capitals of Europe. She was favored of kings, the leading figure in many startling escapades, the toast of Paris. She was a princess, an American princess, who had captured the old world by her wit and her daring as much as by her lovely face.*
>
> *Today she lies dead in her home in Padua, Italy—a prodigal daughter spurned by her mother, shunned by her former companions, her life ended, if not in poverty, at least in unlovely circumstances. She died a woman without illusions.*

DR. HARFFY'S HARPSICHORD

Dr. William Harffy, a British surgeon, left Detroit in 1796 and moved to the Canadian side of the river. He took his junky old harpsichord with him—a decision he came to regret.

"Curse the music. I wish it was sold. I care not for what… You will favor me if it could be in any ways disposed of," Dr. Harffy wrote to a friend on October 17, 1799.

But he couldn't sell it—it was a wreck. So when a friend of his, Commodore Alexander Grant, sailed from Grosse Pointe to Ontario for a visit, Dr. Harffy decided to have a little fun.

He snuck the harpsichord on the boat. It sailed back to Michigan with the commodore. He came to regret this decision, too.

"I really am sorry that the harpsichord was put in Mr. Grant's boat," Dr. Harffy wrote to a mutual friend. "For he talks about it. God, how he talks about it."

The harpsichord was removed to a village storehouse and never heard from again.

Rivalries

When Detroit Republicans decided that they needed a businessman in office in 1889—someone mild, broadly appealing and sensitive to their landed interests—they nominated fifty-year-old gentle giant Hazen Stuart Pingree. Pingree, a Civil War veteran who had been captured by Confederate forces at the Battle of North Anna in 1864, wasn't a political person. But his reverence for President Abraham Lincoln, and the values Lincoln outlined in his address at Gettysburg, inspired Pingree to join the Michigan Republican Club.

His shoe company—started small in 1866 with $1,500, used machinery and eight employees—had grown into a huge operation, grossing upward of $1 million a year. It made Pingree a wealthy man. *Their* wealthy man, Detroit Republicans wagered. They wagered wrong.

When Pingree promised to root out corruption in city contracts and initiate widespread municipal reforms, he wasn't paying lip service to disenchanted Democrats. Pingree was for *real*. After his landslide election to office, he wasted no time.

Within weeks, wheels were in motion. He announced a sweeping plan to repave Detroit's rancid cedar block streets and improve street cleaning. He fought to correct unfairly low tax assessments on high-value property owned by holding companies. And he began a decades-long battle to secure fair play and reasonable rates for public services; Detroiters paid nearly double the rate for their gas and electricity as residents of other cities in Michigan and the Midwest.

Hazen S. Pingree, circa 1900. *Library of Congress, Prints & Photographs Division, Detroit Publishing Company Collection, reproduction no. LC-D4-40050.*

He made enemies everywhere. The Republican Party and members of the business community felt betrayed. Newspapers ignored him. Banks refused to work with him. Old friends stopped talking to him. But the people adored him, and the angrier he made corporate interests, the more they showered him with love.

STREET FIGHTERS

In the same election that made Pingree mayor, fellow Civil War veteran James Vernor was elected to the Detroit Common Council.

As a pharmacy clerk, Vernor had tinkered with a ginger ale recipe on the side. But it just wasn't coming together, so when he enlisted to serve in the Union army in 1862, he dumped his experiment into a wooden cask for safekeeping. He returned home to a lucrative surprise: the barrel-aged soda base had just the right balance of mellow, sweet and spicy. Vernor's—the oldest still-produced soda in the country—was born.

James Vernor Sr., circa 1885. C.M. Hayes & Company. *Burton Historical Collection, Detroit Public Library.*

That's how Vernor liked to tell the story, anyway. While there's no proof of the happy accident that gave the world Vernor's barrel-aged ginger ale, it was, of course, true that Vernor enlisted—he was a member of the Fourth Michigan Cavalry, the unit that captured Confederate president Jefferson Davis at Irwinville, Georgia, in May 1865. Vernor kept a dressing gown and a gold piece that had belonged to Davis as souvenirs.

Like Pingree, Vernor was briefly a prisoner of war, but he escaped his captors and hid in an abandoned house for three days while the Union army drove Confederates out of Murfreesboro, Tennessee.

Vernor, too, went into business when he returned from the war, opening a pharmacy and soda shop on Woodward Avenue in 1866—the same year that Pingree started his shoe company. And like Pingree, Vernor's enterprising spirit made him rich.

In 1889, Detroit streetcars were still pulled by horses and heated by smelly stoves, their carriage floors covered with straw. Most cities of Detroit's size had long since electrified their rail lines. The streetcars paid no property taxes to the city for the privilege of running their services on its streets. They were supposed to pay 1 percent of gross revenue instead, but they refused to let the city inspect the books and paid whatever they felt appropriate.

Vernor had spent years standing in the doorway of his drugstore, greeting his neighbors and customers, tipping his hat to passersby and watching horses—so many horses!—hauling taxis, grocery stands and well-heeled ladies riding in rickety two-wheeled carts.

A lot of old-timers of Vernor's generation went on record lamenting the loss of the slow, charmed tranquility of pre-industrial Detroit, with its sleepy streets, big trees and quirky French habits. Not Vernor. Sure, he was a little old-fashioned. When his brother moved a little far from the city center, Vernor warned him of Indian raids. He wore his Civil War–era side-whiskers for his entire life. But for the most part, Vernor was ready for the future. The reason he ended up in politics in the first place was because he wanted a better sewer on the street near his business—the damn thing was always flooding his basement. He wanted to get rid of the dusty old farmers' market in Cadillac Square—a provincial throwback and haven for ne'er-do-wells—and implement modern reforms.

So when the streetcar issue came up in the council—when Mayor Pingree called for electric lines, a three-cent fare and an end to private monopoly—Vernor understood. He knew the importance of modernizing Detroit and keeping pace with the thrumming national metropolis Detroit was about to become. Vernor wanted streetcar improvements. He just didn't think that the city would do a very good job of improving them.

Meanwhile, streetcar employees were organizing and agitating. Drivers were asking for a ten-hour workday (to replace the standard twelve-hour split-shift), but employees who threatened to unionize were in turn threatened with wage cuts or summary dismissal. On April 21, 1891, streetcar workers went on strike. Curious spectators became angered sympathizers at the sight of a strikebreaker with a gun who was threatening to shoot anyone blocking the line.

A mêlée ensued. "Silk-gloved and plug-hatted men, side by side of horny-handed, mud-bespattered, unkempt men, vied with each other in tearing up the tracks," wrote one observer.

In one of those potent Detroit-making stories we tell over and over again—like the baker with the pony knocking his pipe on his boot and burning down the city—U.S. Postmaster General Don M. Dickinson led a mob down Woodward Avenue in hauling a streetcar and heaving it into the river.

Despite pleas from prominent citizens, Pingree refused to call in state troops. In a speech at the scene of the unrest, Pingree encouraged workers to negotiate with their employers. To the employers, he suggested terms of arbitration—shorter hours, higher pay—that were reluctantly accepted.

Back at city hall, the streetcar company promised that plans were about to get underway for a sweeping electrification project—if only the city would grant it another thirty-year franchise. No property taxes; no increase in revenue sharing. Just the pinky-swear that there would for sure be an upgrade. The Common Council approved the request. Mayor Pingree promptly vetoed it.

Coupled with the strike—which curried abundant public favor for the streetcar unions and for Pingree—it was the starting shot (no actual bullets fired, thankfully) in what pundits would come to call the Thirty Years' War for control of the streetcar system.

In 1893, while the extension of the private streetcar deal was tied up in the courts, Vernor led a special committee of the Common Council to negotiate a franchise for the Detroit Citizens Street Railway (contrary to what the name suggests, it was owned by some deep-pocketed investors from New York). It passed, but Pingree vetoed this, too—the fare system was too high. He had promised the citizenry a three-cent streetcar. And Pingree, as he continued to show, kept his promises.

Pingree had been dead for twenty years when the Thirty Years' War finally came to an end. In 1921, under Mayor James Couzens, the city finally took control of the streetcar system.

Vernor—who would serve on the Common Council for twenty-five years—reversed his stance on public ownership. As he avowed that he had been wrong about private ownership all those years ago, he voted to approve a municipal takeover.

But for the rest of the time they worked in Old City Hall together, a chill settled between Alderman Vernor and Mayor Pingree. Though they had been friends, business peers and brothers in war, the wedge of progress—and how to achieve it—separated them in politics, and Vernor never walked warmly into Pingree's office again.

Today, Vernor is mostly remembered for his soda, although in obituaries at the time of his death, his famous ginger ale is a footnote to his expansive career in city government during a time of flux.

Pingree is remembered as a fighter, a reformer and a take-no-prisoners progressive. And he is remembered by his monument in Grand Circus Park—just across Woodward Avenue from a memorial to another Pingree rival.

ETERNAL RIVALS

In 1897, after three terms as mayor, Hazen Pingree packed for Lansing to serve as governor of Michigan. (He had tried to persuade the courts that he could hold both offices at the same time, that feisty so-and-so.)

Pingree wanted to leave his office in Detroit to a handpicked Republican successor, Captain Albert Stewart, a Great Lakes sailor who acted and spoke like one. He promised to do in office "whatever the governor tells me to do."

Captain Stewart lost the election to William Cotter Maybury, a Democrat "famed if not for inventing, at least perfecting the art of going through the neighborhoods kissing babies," wrote Malcolm Bingay. Maybury was a mustachioed gentleman bachelor-lawyer who had served two terms as a U.S. representative.

In Lansing, Pingree struggled to pass meaningful reform measures, blocked at every turn by a cabal of unmoveable senators that came to be known as "the Immortal Nineteen." His street-level, sweat-and-shirtsleeves tactics—like the potato patch plan, which turned vacant lots into pocket gardens to help the urban poor stave off starvation, or the time he marched into a school board meeting and arrested four of the board members on corruption charges—made him a walking monument to progress in Detroit. But Old Ping couldn't gain any traction at the capitol.

Back in Detroit, Maybury made excellent speeches and planned a magnificent bicentennial celebration, with parades, floats, pageants and feather plumes. He was genial and pro-business and tried not to rock the boat. Detroiters thought he was a pretty nice guy.

Pingree decided to retire at the end of his second term. On December 31, 1899, he cleared out all of the seats from the House floor and threw a huge New Year's Eve/Turn of the Century party. Future president Teddy Roosevelt came dressed in his Rough Riders uniform. Revelers stayed up until dawn, making speeches and toasting their outgoing governor—who, it's only natural, was planning a grand retirement big-game hunt in Africa. You know…to unwind.

He never made it home from the safari. He fell ill with dysentery on the hunt, was rushed to London and died there, despite the emergency care of King Edward VII's own physicians. He was sixty.

As soon as news crossed the wire in Detroit, the city slipped into grief. Mourning bunting draped city hall with banners reading, "Ambitious. Fearless. Staunch. True." And then a funny thing happened: people started calling the newspaper offering five-, ten- and twenty-five-cent contributions for a monument to Pingree's memory.

Four years later, a statue of Pingree, perched at the edge of a chair, his foot overhanging the pedestal, like he's ready to leap into action, was

Hazen S. Pingree Monument in Grand Circus Park, circa 1905. Sculpture by Rudolph Schwarz, unveiled in 1904. *Burton Historical Collection, Detroit Public Library.*

William Cotter
Maybury Monument.
Sculpture by Adolph
Alexander Weinman,
unveiled 1912. *Photo by
the author.*

unveiled at Grand Circus Park. More than five thousand people donated to build the statue.

When William Cotter Maybury died in 1909, his friend and former police commissioner George W. Fowles proposed a public monument to the late mayor across Grand Circus Park from the lurching Pingree memorial. The public was unenthused, so Fowles and some of his friends from the Maybury administration and the business community quietly, privately raised $20,000 to build one anyway. It was unveiled in 1912.

Adversaries in life, they are entrenched in a never-ending showdown in Detroit's oldest park. But while Pingree looks stalwartly up Woodward Avenue, William C. Maybury holds a different gaze: across the wide boulevard, toward Pingree, as if wondering, "What made *him* so special?"

THE ARCHBISHOP

Inever used to second-guess memorial statues. You know the type: tall, bronze and handsome and sometimes on a horse. If you watch for them when you're traveling, you start to see the same faces: Thaddeus Kosciuszko, Robert Burns, Dante, Leif Ericson, Joan of Arc and pretty much every Civil War general ever.

Then I met Jim Scott. And now I always wonder.

Who was this man of mystery—Detroit's "boss romancer," raconteur and prankster millionaire? And why does he have a larger-than-life statue—and to match, a gleaming marble fountain, like something from a Cecil B. DeMille set—in his honor?

Let's start from the top. James Scott was born on December 20, 1831, in a house on Woodward Avenue. Though his early life was not without hardship—his mother died before he turned three and his father when Jim was a teenager—Scott was born wealthy, and he never had to work too hard. His father, John Scott, had come to Detroit penniless and spent years on construction contracts, investing in land and building wealth; he retired into public service. By that example, Jim Scott's chosen path in life was doubly irritating to the virtuous entrepreneurs of this make-it-yourself town.

When he was twenty-five, he started a gambling hall for faro players—and, with it, a reputation that followed him to his death and beyond. Was he a gambler? No one is sure, but it's likely. Of course, in the 1850s, Detroit was "wide open," as Robert B. Ross defended in 1905:

Drinking was the rule…In the best houses, decanters of wine, brandy and whiskey always stood on the sideboards. Gambling was not only tolerated, but cultivated…Almost every business man held the opinion that gambling increased the prosperity of a city…The average gambler was well-dressed, polite, generous and a good story-teller…and scrupulously honest.

Well, maybe. Faro was wildly popular in American frontier towns. It was also notorious. "In an honest game of Faro splits should occur about three times in two deals," according to *The Fireside Book of Cards.*

"But an honest game has always been a great rarity; faro was a cheating business almost from the time of its invention."

Yes, the mayor asked Scott to shut down his gambling hall for a while. But it was only because some of his clientele were making unwelcome comments to ladies on the street—wasn't it?

Scott seemed to edit his own biography as he lived it. Was he really a millionaire? Some said he was; to them, Scott said, "Prove it," and no one could. Why did he leave for St. Louis? What did he do when he was there? Rumors spread that he lost a huge chunk of his personal fortune in a rigged game of faro and forswore gambling forever. Others noticed a few new diamond rings on his fingers when he returned to

The life-size monument to Jim Scott erected with his grand Italianate fountain. The artist hoped that no one would recognize him without a top hat. Sculpture by Herbert Adams, 1925. *Photo by the author.*

Detroit and raised their eyebrows. Scott liked to brag about his high-rolling years on the Mississippi, winning jackpots and outrunning the police, but his associates, including former Detroit mayor John C. Lodge, privately confessed that Scott was too cheap to gamble even a nickel on the likelihood that the sun would rise.

Scott favored white bow ties, ruffled shirts and, long after they were out of style, tall beaver top hats. Because of his long black beard, he was sometimes called "the Archbishop," but his flamboyant sense of fashion is not what made his reputation. At the city's tony hotel bars and social clubs, Scott held court, drinking and telling long-winded, ribald and apparently insufferable jokes.

The *Detroit Tribune* ran a profile of Scott, "Detroit's boss romancer," in its March 14, 1885 edition:

> *He never tells the same story twice, and does not depend on traveling men for his stock of stories, but invents them himself. He tells lots of funny things in different dialects…There is one friend of Jim's, however, who insists that he dishes up old chestnuts, and when this friend sees the joker coming, he runs and hides in the hay-mow.*

How bad were his jokes? Here's one of them, paraphrased from the same article: Two friends take a recently dead guy to the bar with them. Then they leave the dead guy at the bar when it's time to pay their tab. The bartender gets mad that the dead guy won't pay, and he punches the dead guy in the head. The corpse falls to the floor. And then the two scofflaws run back inside the bar and say, "Oh, my God! You killed him!" And the bartender says, "So what if I did? He pulled a knife on me first."

Beyond the barroom, too, Scott had a distinctive sense of humor—or a delirious sense of spite, depending on whose books you read. In 1891, construction began on Jim Scott's masterstroke of mean wit: the Folly.

When the neighbor next to Scott's lot at Park and Peterboro refused to sell—quoting him an exorbitant price—Scott had a mansion built that rivaled all the rest on the block. But only from the front. In the back of the house—the side facing the neighbor—the mansion was nothing but a brick wall, three stories high, blotting out the sunlight and replacing a view of the boulevard with an ugly façade.

Scott never lived in the house. He didn't rent it. He wouldn't sell it. He just left it. But he took pride in personally mowing the lawn. Wrote Ross: "This is the only manual labor he ever did in his life."

But was he a venomous cad? Or just a merry prankster? Some evidence suggests that Scott had cast himself in the role of a "witty sport," and his hijinks occasionally garnered a corner or two of a national newspaper—perhaps Scott was experimenting with what we'd call "personal branding" today. It was rumored that he was actually quite generous when no one was looking; waiters loved him for his lavish tips, and he had a yearly competition with innkeeper Seymour Finney to see who could file his city taxes in the timeliest manner.

One reporter caught Scott delivering fruit and blankets to a family who'd lost their home in a fire. The lead: "Even the heart of the meanest man in town had been touched." When the story ran the next day, Scott called the editor in a rage, demanding that the paper issue a retraction for the "attack on his character." Was he worried that a story of his soft, thoughtful center would sully his "surly jester" image?

Reprehensible lout or harmless rich eccentric, we wouldn't be asking these questions if Scott had died quietly—by now he would be lost to history. But Scott saw to it that Detroiters like us would be debating the old wise guy's finer points of personality more than a century later.

It's either the most outrageous act of self-aggrandizement in city history or the greatest last laugh in public art. When Clarence M. Burton—with his lawyer hat on—executed Scott's will in 1910, he shared the shocking news with the world: Scott had left most of his $600,000 estate to the city for a grand fountain on Belle Isle. The catch? The city also had to build a statue of Jim Scott.

The controversy was immediate. Scott was not a well-liked man; he had no friends, and no one had any good reason to stick up for him. The shady dean of the faro house, litigious prankster, teller of off-color jokes and cane-shaker at neighborhood kids? A man whose highest aim in life seemed to be aggravating as many people as possible? How could the city in good conscience celebrate the memory of such a rake?

The churchy contingent marched out first against the fountain, naturally. The man *drank*, for heaven's sake. From the temperance movement's perspective, which once again dominated Detroit's moral conversation (in less than ten years, prohibition would be the law of the land), the life of Jim Scott looked pretty depraved, almost like a missed opportunity—a soul that had not been saved. "Only a good man who has wrought things for humanity should be honored in this way," said Bishop Charles D. Williams.

People who spent their whole lives building fortunes from scratch resented Scott and his fountain, too. J.L. Hudson, immigrant and department store magnate, put it a little more plainly: the fountain would be "a monument to nastiness and filthy stories. Mr. Scott never did anything for Detroit in his lifetime, and he never had a thought that was good for the city."

Except, of course, for the fountain. Leaving your colossal estate to the city for a public works project—that counts for something, right?

And that's exactly the tack taken by his few, but famous, defenders. Like former senator Thomas W. Palmer, a city sage at eighty years old, who stood before the Common Council and shared a memory of Scott, just a vulnerable boy in a schoolyard. Hands shaking, he spun a dreamy parable about a man who grew up without a mother or a YMCA, and though he'd squandered his life on malicious pursuits, he faced mortality and found that boyish hope still alive in the pit of his person, thereafter resolving to right his life and leave something that the young men and women of Detroit could enjoy forever.

Grandiose, certainly. Even remotely true—who could ever say? But the old senator, maybe just because he was so old, touched hearts that day.

Others, like Alderman David Heineman, rightly pointed out that most members of the Common Council had no business throwing stones at Scott's character: "I can look around this office and see pictures of men who played poker with Jim Scott. I say the bequest should be accepted."

The Common Council referred the matter to committee, which reported in December 1910 that after public meetings and discussions with Scott's acquaintances, it was determined that

> those objecting have been misled as to the occupation and character of the deceased….Not a single voice accused or even intimated in the slightest degree that he was dishonest or ever attempted to wilfully or knowingly wrong any one; no one questions his integrity, and his occupation was that sought by ninety-five percent of the American people, a "retired

capitalist"…The only thing which is pointed to as being against him are the follies of youth, and those he discarded over 40 years ago.

Opined the *New York Times* on January 29, 1911, when it shared the news that the impasse had been resolved:

This is the story of a man who led a practically blameless life for eighty years, according to the preponderance of testimony, as blameless as that of the average man at least, who loved his home, his family, his friends, and his city, the latter so much that when he died he left five-sixths of a fortune of $600,000 to the municipality of Detroit with which to build a fountain on Belle Isle, and who has been since his death, a year ago, unmercifully reviled for his generosity. James Scott was his name—"Jim" he was universally called.

The fountain, and its matching monument to an otherwise unimportant man, was a go. In the years between Scott's death and the start of construction, the estate he left the city rocketed in value to more than $1 million, and the scope of the project grew with it. When it was finished, the project had changed the very landscape of Belle Isle's west end; the fountain concourse was elevated so water could cascade into a 500-foot-long reflecting pool. Cass Gilbert, architect of the U.S. Supreme Court building, designed a Neoclassical marvel with a central water jet capable of 125-foot sprays, liberally adorned with spitting Neptunes, stately lions, turtles, dolphins, maidens and a fountain bowl lined with handmade-in-Detroit Pewabic pottery tiles.

The statue of Jim Scott is, indeed, larger than life—not two and a half feet tall, as one fountain detractor suggested, nor made of soap. He is not wearing a hat, which some hoped would make the relentlessly top-hatted Scott unrecognizable. He does not have the majestic view of the city he had hoped for: he is shadowed by the fountain's grandeur, and few visitors today know or care who he is.

But the Archbishop's fountain is, indisputably, a gem. Children play in it. Photographers take pictures of it. Couples get married in front of it, and at night it lights up like a firework.

And for that, you can almost see Jim Scott smirking. The joke, once and for all, is on us.

Burying the Boy Governor

Every time Detroit feels young again, we turn to the Boy Governor. Just nineteen when President Andrew Jackson appointed him secretary of the Michigan Territory and only twenty-five when he became acting governor, Stevens Thomson Mason is a handsome touchstone for anyone in a youthful, voracious mood. And he was the perfect first governor for a capital city perpetually on the brink of a massive shift.

Every generation dredges up his memory. Most generations have also dredged up his casket.

Decisive, charismatic, unapologetic and committed to the Union but dedicated to the autonomy and prosperity of Michigan, Stevens T. Mason was a once-in-a-lifetime leader. He was such a threat to order in Washington that Jackson removed him from office.

With a stubborn temperament, a fine sense of style and, above all, the support of the territory's fiercely loyal citizens, Mason saw Michigan through a war with Ohio over the Toledo strip and straight to statehood.

Mason's first term as Michigan's first governor was a less fortunate affair. His administration had borrowed millions of dollars to fund canals, railroads and other internal improvements. When the Panic of 1837 derailed the economy—and bankrupted both the canal company and the bank backing the loans—Michigan sank into debt. Governor Mason knew that his political career was done for, and he chose not to run for reelection in 1839. Disgraced, he left the state to start a private law practice in New York.

Stevens T. Mason, from a painting at Memorial Hall, University of Michigan, circa 1900–1910. *Library of Congress, Prints & Photographs Division, Detroit Publishing Company Collection, LC-D416-554.*

Business never really picked up. Then, after a New Year's Eve party, Mason fell ill with pneumonia. On January 4, 1843, in the middle of the night, he died. He was thirty-one years old.

His anguished father, John T. Mason, wrote to his daughter, Kate, with the news of her brother's death:

> *Your beloved brother is no more—I cannot yet realize the awful truth. But it is nevertheless so. He now lies a corpse in this house. His sickness was not considered dangerous until two hours before his death, and it was so sudden, so calm and so free from pain that to look upon him at this moment the serenity of his countenance cheats you into the belief that he still lives. Yes! He does, but in another world, the destined abode of us all.*

News reached Detroit a week later, and on Sunday, January 15, 1843, the city observed a day of mourning and held a huge (though wholly symbolic) "funeral" for their Boy Governor at the church he had attended on Woodward Avenue. Thousands of mourners and spectators crowded narrow wooden sidewalks to watch the biggest funeral parade the city had ever seen: a silent, casket-less procession of military guards, the governor, the mayor, senators, representatives, aldermen, judges and members of the bar.

He was buried in New York, where he lay peacefully at rest for sixty-two years. It was the longest his earthly remains would stay in one place for the next two centuries.

REINTERMENT, 1905

By the 1880s, the fate of Marble Cemetery—on Second Avenue in New York City's East Village—was uncertain. You know the story: crowded conditions, valuable land and absentee owners. Rumors circulated that the city might buy it to build a school. Muckracker, photographer and social reformer Jacob Riis thought that it would be a good place for a playground. But the owners had to agree to any changes—and the owners were nowhere to be found. A nearly successful attempt to dissolve the cemetery organization in 1905 worried plot owners, who began to make arrangements for relatives to be disinterred and taken elsewhere.

Back in Detroit, Lawton T. Hemans, an amateur historian and self-appointed steward of Stevens T. Mason's fading legacy, feared that the cemetery would be destroyed with one of Detroit's best and brightest still buried in his Tuckahoe marble vault. Hemans, rather remarkably, tracked down Mason's living relatives—his elderly sister, Emily, and his daughter, Dorothea—who agreed that the governor's body belonged to Detroit. Hemans appealed to progressive Michigan governor and former cheese magnate Fred Warner, who sympathized with the cause. Warner appointed Hemans to a committee to oversee the affair.

On June 4, 1905, at 9:15 a.m., the train carrying the mahogany casket of Stevens T. Mason arrived in Detroit. It had chugged across the Great Lakes region on a railroad line that Mason, as governor, had chartered. Warner and the Detroit Light Guard greeted the party at the station, where Mason's casket was draped in an American flag and blanketed with lilies and greenery.

Crowds pressed for a look at the belle of the hour, Emily Virginia Mason, as she disembarked the train. Lively at ninety, the governor's

Fetching Emily V. Mason sent this New Year's postcard to her "old friend" Clarence M. Burton about 1900, apologizing that she could not find a more recent photograph of herself. *Burton Historical Collection, Detroit Public Library.*

younger sister embodied the mythic, bygone grace and southern gentility that the Masons brought to muddy Detroit. Stevens was a bachelor while he was in office, so at eighteen years old, boarding school–educated Emily became a sort of first lady—entertainer, captain of the house and caretaker to the sometimes unkempt governor, who had a habit of skipping dinner and staying up late to study.

A charming society lady in her own right, she attended countless balls, courted beaus and let chivalrous men place their handkerchiefs over puddles so she would not have to soil her dainty boots (or so General Friend Palmer once witnessed).

After Mason left office, Emily left Detroit for travels with her diplomat father in New Orleans, her native Virginia and Cherokee country in Arkansas. A close friend of General Robert E. Lee, Emily Mason nursed soldiers at Confederate hospitals during the Civil War. Some called her the Florence Nightingale of the Confederacy. After the war, she went to Paris for fifteen years to work at an American school for girls. She also wrote a biography of Lee and compiled a book of Southern war poetry. Her "old friends" in Detroit—most of whom must have been just children when Emily lived there, if they had been born at all—were thrilled to see her.

From the station, the Light Guard loaded the casket into a horse-drawn hearse bound for the armory on Larned Avenue. It was set on a bier covered by a purple cloth and bedecked by palms and evergreens. In the next ninety minutes, two thousand people filed through to pay their respects.

That was about the size of the city when Mason was governor. In 1905, the population neared a half million. Outside the armory, thousands more people lined the streets and waited through the service.

It began with a benediction by Reverend David M. Cooper and an opening address by Mayor George P. Codd. Governor Warner gave a long speech—by a few accounts, it was a snoozer. Clarence M. Burton, the keynote speaker, shared a brief history of Mason's life and his expansive influence on the fate of the state. Lawton Hemans read a letter Stevens wrote to Emily just weeks before he died that shared his late-winter dream of a summer vacation to Detroit.

Finally, Cooper asked to say a few more words. Shaky and tearful, he took the podium. When he was a boy, he confessed—upon seeing Governor Mason descending the capitol steps in Detroit with his white cloak and gold-tipped cane—that Cooper had shouted at him, "Five-quarters!" an insult of the day about the governor's salary. Cooper didn't know what it meant; he'd just heard his father say it at the dinner table.

The first state capitol, later Capitol Union High School, circa 1870. *Burton Historical Collection, Detroit Public Library.*

In fear of his big cane, I climbed up the Capitol steps—I was brave enough not to run away—and the governor turned and followed me. I was astonished when he walked up to me, put his arms around my neck and, for five minutes, gave me the sweetest, most fatherly talk imaginable. I cannot remember one word of what he said, but that impression has remained with me ever since, and I have never ceased to love the man and his memory.

When Mason was governor, the capitol had been so far removed from town that the road didn't even go there—at Congress Street, Griswold became a dirt footpath. In 1847, the capital was moved to Lansing; the original capitol building then served as the city high school until it burned down in 1893. In 1905, the site was a slice of grass in the middle of the city called, somewhat hopefully, Capitol Park.

After the service, the First Regiment band began to play, and the processional—led by a cortege of mounted police on black horses and thronged by thousands—headed that way.

Under the salute of the state and American flags, as a band played "Michigan, My Michigan," Stevens T. Mason was laid to rest where he had once led a wild territory to the brink of greatness.

Wrote the *Detroit Free Press*:

Today the casket containing the remains of Michigan's first Governor lies beneath the foundation walls of the building which saw the greater portion of those victories—the old State Capitol. Both the man and the structure are crumbled into dust, but neither are forgotten, and their influence is still felt in the every day life of Michigan.

Mason was home. In the history of Detroiters celebrating and solemnizing Detroit's history, this was the city's proudest and most tender moment. The city hall bells tolled all day.

REINTERMENT, 1955

A few years after his grand homecoming, a jaunty statue of Stevens T. Mason—made from melted-down Fort Michilimackinac cannons—marked

Stevens T. Mason statue, sculpture by
Albert Weinert, 1908. Capitol Park, Detroit,
Michigan. *Photo by the author.*

the spot of the Boy Governor's grave in Capitol Park. Chin up and dapper,
it surveyed the modest memorial park as the city around it shape-shifted.

When Kent Sagendorph published his biography of Mason in 1947,
Capitol Park had grown shaded and shabby, and no one seemed to
remember why it was there:

> *Visitors to Detroit seldom include Capitol Park among the modern
> attractions of the great motor metropolis. Mason is there; his body lies
> beneath the statue and his monument towers above. He stands there,
> erect and dashing as he was in life, but the huge skyscrapers of midtown
> Detroit dwarf the little triangular space and let in little light. The bronze
> figure seems tiny now, and hard to find even if one looks for it. Bushes
> have grown up, untrimmed, almost to the statue's shoulder. On either
> side of the bushes are enormous comfort-station signs, which get most of
> the attention. Impatient cars line the curbs, bumper to bumper. Mounted
> police-men on imperious steeds glare at taxi drivers, who glare back.
> There stands Mason, forever glancing straight down Griswold with an
> expression of amused tolerance, but few of the thousands who pass there
> daily have ever noticed his monument…Whirls of dust and bits of paper
> and gum wrappers blow unnoticed around Mason's calm, boyish face.*

Since people were already using it for the purpose, in 1955 the city decided to make it official and redesign Capitol Park as a transit center, with a major bus interchange and four new convenience stations. Mason would have to be reinterred.

Living descendants—especially Marie Louise Anderson, Mason's great-grandniece—agreed that it was time for Mason's remains to be taken to Lansing. On July 15, 1955, a legislative committee in Lansing voted to bring the state's first governor to the state capitol, where he would be buried with appropriate solemnity and a fitting memorial dedicated. Detroit wasn't having it. City Council president Louis Miriani called it a "boondoggle."

Newspapers had already reported that Mason was not long for Detroit, but on August 2, the Detroit Common Council voted to reinter Mason in Capitol Park—and quickly, before anyone could pick a fight about it. Legislators in Lansing were annoyed with Miriani's bravado, and the governor's office was perplexed and disappointed, but no one wanted to get mixed up in a historical territory brawl with Detroit.

Anderson was furious. Though previously polite in her correspondence, she wrote an exasperated letter to Detroit mayor Albert Cobo:

> *I, for one, am utterly opposed to having him re-buried in that noisy little park surrounded by office buildings and bus loading stations for mostly foreign-born citizens, who have no time or inclination to stop or read. If he cannot rest in a consecrated cemetery, at least he would have room and dignity and quiet resting place on the State Capitol grounds in Lansing…*
>
> *If he is reburied in that dinky little park, he will not be exhumed soon again to put him in a proper place, but he will have to be removed again eventually, when the city is finally obliged to obliterate that little triangle in the path of progress.*

But Miriani would make no apologies. On August 18, 1955, he wrote to Anderson:

> *As one born in Detroit, I learned at an early age its history and traditions, and especially the story of its first governor, the forceful and courageous*

Stevens T. Mason. Since Detroit was his capital, it would seem to be appropriate that his remains rest in a nice setting in our city.

We are spending better than one hundred thousand dollars to beautify Capitol Park, and for that reason I voted to keep the remains of Michigan's first governor here.

Mason was reinterred on December 5, 1955, in a small, brief ceremony in Capitol Park. The service, though originally scheduled for 4:00 p.m., had to be moved to 2:00 p.m. to accommodate for traffic congestion.

Anderson's prophecy that progress would wipe away Capitol Park has not come to pass so far. But she was right about one thing: he had to be removed again, eventually.

REINTERMENT, 2010

Something scary happened in 2010: we thought we lost the governor.

Big plans for Capitol Park were announced in 2009. After decades of neglect, the Detroit Economic Growth Corporation launched a redesign and redevelopment effort in the area to improve the park, attract business and give the governor and his oxidized, bird waste–bespotted monument a little sprucing up.

Yes, they would need to remove his remains. Again. But the project hit a snag when, in June 2010, word spread that work crews didn't find the governor where they thought he would be.

Were they looking for an urn of ashes? A cement tomb with a coffin inside? No one could say for certain—even though the funeral company that had performed the 1955 exhumation was again contracted for the work in 2010.

The whole city (or just every history nerd in the city) watched anxiously as a work crew searched. And honestly, it was as good a chance as any for Detroiters to get reacquainted with the story of Stevens T. Mason, the astonishing young man who became governor of the expansive Michigan Territory and fought even the most dauntless opponents (looking at you, Andrew Jackson) for Michigan's right, by the people's will, to incorporate as a state.

After four gripping days, the crew uncovered the Boy Governor's steel casket. Michigan exhaled. He was reinterred on October 27, 2010—his 199th birthday—in an above-ground vault beneath his statue.

Mason's tomb, for generations, has served as a stark study of history in the path of progress. But a community and its history need to coexist. No, more than that: a community should be able to stand on its history and use it to gain momentum and push forward.

For the small ceremony, attended mostly by journalists, the Michigan Historical Society recruited a contingent of young Detroit leaders to serve as honorary pallbearers.

I was there, too. (I mean, of course I was.) Looking up at the dashing Boy Governor, I had to shield my eyes from the sun, and even though it was windy, it was warm enough to take off my coat. Pigeons circled. Senior citizens in the assisted living residence across the street sat in folding chairs on the balcony.

It would be ridiculous to say that Mason would not recognize the Detroit that holds Capitol Park in its heart today. Neither would Marie Louise Anderson. Neither would Governor Warner or Clarence Burton or the Fifth Regiment Marine Corps or Gabriel Richard. People call up the mythical Detroit That Was with such tragedy, as if Silas Farmer would kneel at the site of the long-destroyed city hall (now the site of a fluid, glassy downtown office building) and weep. Well, maybe he would. We don't know.

But I hope, even believe, that he would not. Sure, Detroit is different now. Damaged, certainly. There are things about this city that tie my stomach in knots. But the lesson of Detroit, I believe, is that it perseveres. That its dynamism is part of its character. And that again and again, against the dirtiest odds, it will rise from the ashes.

Stevens T. Mason and his little triangle park, leafy above the buried ruins of the first state capitol, are still in the middle of a big city—one that rarely thinks of him. Trash still blows through Capitol Park. Kids skateboard there. Downtown employees wander through it without a thought to Mason's life or legacy.

But it's good to know that he's there when you need him. When times call for decisive action, tremendous courage or—especially—the energy of a fearless, youthful heart, Stevens T. Mason stands at the ready, silently rallying his public.

SELECTED BIBLIOGRAPHY

Austin, Dan. "Hazen S. Pingree Monument." HistoricDetroit.org, 2011.

Bates, George C. "By-Gones of Old Detroit." Historical Collections of the Michigan Pioneer and Historical Society, vol. 22, 1894.

Bingay, Malcolm. *Detroit Is My Own Hometown.* New York: Bobbs-Merrill Company, 1946.

Burton, Clarence M. *A Sketch of the Life of Antoine Cadillac.* Detroit, MI: Wilton-Smith, 1895.

———. *When Detroit Was Young: Historical Studies.* Detroit, MI: Burton Abstract and Title Company, 1953.

Burton, Patricia Owens. *Clarence Monroe Burton: Detroit's Historian.* Detroit, MI: Burton Abstract and Title Company, 1957.

Campbell, Honorable James V. "Biographical Sketch of Charles Christopher Trowbridge." Pioneer Society of the State of Michigan, Pioneer Collections, vol. 6, 1884. Reprinted, 1907.

Catlin, George. *The Story of Detroit.* Detroit, MI: Evening News Association, 1926.

Conot, Robert. *American Odyssey.* New York: William Morrow & Company, 1974.

Detroit Post. "The Best-Lighted City in the World: Detroit Streets." August 20, 1883. Reprinted in the *New York Times*, August 26, 1885.

Detroit Post & Tribune. "Detroit Half a Century Ago: Interesting Letters Written From and About Detroit—Some Predictions, and How They Have Been Fulfilled." November 9, 1872.

Dunbar, Willis F., and George S. May. *Michigan: A History of the Wolverine State.* Grand Rapids, MI: Wm. B. Edermans Publishing Company, 1995.

Farmer, Silas. *Guide and Souvenir of Detroit: With Maps and Illustrations.* Detroit, MI: Silas Farmer & Company, 1891.

———. *History of Detroit and Michigan, or: The Metropolis Illustrated.* Detroit, MI: Silas Farmer & Company, 1884.

Gavrilovich, Peter, and Bill McGraw, eds. *The Detroit Almanac: 300 Years of Life in the Motor City.* Detroit, MI: Detroit Free Press, 2000.

Hamlin, Carrie. "Old French Traditions." Report of the Pioneer Society of the State of Michigan, vol. 4, 1883.

Hendrickson, Wilma Wood, ed. *Detroit Perspectives: Crossroads and Turning Points.* Detroit, MI: Wayne State University Press, 1991.

Hoskins, Ronald G. "Walker, Hiram." *Dictionary of Canadian Biography Online*, vol. 12. http://www.biographi.ca/009004-119.01-e.php?BioId=40606.

Labadie, Jo. "Cranky Notions." *Motorman and Conductor* 31, no. 12 (November 1923).

Langguth, A.J. *Union 1812*. New York: Simon & Schuster, 2006.

Marryat, Frederick, Captain. *A Diary in America, with Remarks on Its Institutions.* Philadelphia, PA: Carey & Hart, 1839. Compiled in the Clarke Historical Library online exhibition, I Arrived at Detroit. clarke.cmich.edu.

Marsh, Florence, and Harriet Marsh. *History of Detroit for Young People.* Detroit, MI: privately printed, 1935.

Palmer, Friend. *Early Days in Detroit.* Detroit, MI: Hunt & June, 1906.

Parker, A.A. (Amos Andrew). *Trip to the West and Texas: Comprising a Journey of Eight Thousand Miles, through New-York, Michigan, Illinois, Missouri, Louisiana and Texas, in the Autumn and Winter of 1834–5: Interspersed with Anecdotes, Incidents and Observations.* Concord, New Hampshire, 1835. From Michigana: Sources in U.S. History Online.

Ross, Robert B., and George Catlin. *Landmarks of Detroit.* Detroit, MI: Evening News Association, 1898.

Sagendorph, Kent. *Stevens Thomson Mason: Misunderstood Patriot.* New York: E.P. Dutton, 1947.

Stark, George Washington. *City of Destiny.* Detroit, MI: Arnold-Powers, Inc., 1943.

Taylor, George, Reverend. "First Visit to Michigan: Some Incidents Connected with Early Methodism in the State." Pioneer Society of the State of Michigan, vol. 6, 1884. Reprinted 1907. Accessed at the Internet Archive, archive.org.

Tossy, L.R. "Labor Day Observance: Detroit, Mich." *American Federationist* 3, no. 8 (October 1896).

Tuttle, Charles Richard. *General History of the State of Michigan.* Detroit, MI: R.D.S. Tyler & Company, 1873.

Utley, Henry M., and Byron M. Cutcheon. *Michigan as a Province, Territory and State: The Twenty-sixth Member of the Federal Union.* New York: Publishing Society of Michigan, 1906.

Willard, Frances Elizabeth. *A Wheel within a Wheel: How I Learned to Ride the Bicycle.* London: Hutchinson & Company, 1895.

Woodford, Frank. *Lewis Cass: The Last Jeffersonian.* Piscataway, NJ: Rutgers University Press, 1950.

Woodford, Frank, and Albert Hyma. *Gabriel Richard: Frontier Ambassador.* Detroit, MI: Wayne State University Press, 1958.

Zoltvany, Yves S. "Laumet, *dit* de la Mothe Cadillac, Antoine." *Dictionary of Canadian Biography Online*, vol. 2. http://www.biographi.ca/009004-119.01-e.php?&id_nbr=888.

Burton Historical Collection

Reading Room Files: Biographical Materials, Excerpts and Miscellany

Antoine de la Mothe Cadillac.
Clarence Monroe Burton.
Silas Farmer.
Emily Virginia Mason.
Stevens T. Mason.
Friend Palmer.
James Scott.

Daniel Scotten.
James Vernor Sr.

Also, search by the following:
Local History—Detroit—Cemeteries.
Local History—Detroit—Historic Homes and Haunts.
Local History—Detroit—Pavement.
Local History—Detroit—Saloons.

MANUSCRIPTS

John Askin Papers.
Clarence Burton Scrapbooks.
Felix Meier Papers.
Friend Palmer Scrapbooks.
John Thomson Mason Papers.
William Woodbridge Papers.

ABOUT THE AUTHOR

A my Elliott Bragg blogs about Detroit
history at nighttraintodetroit.com. A
native Detroiter, she left home for a while to
edit an arts and culture magazine and to learn
new media skills in Milwaukee. She returned
to Detroit in 2009 where she lives with her
husband, freelances as a writer, editor and
content manager and works hard at old books.

Visit us at
www.historypress.net